A COMMUNICATIVE APPROACH TO
THE TOEIC® L&R TEST
Book 2: Intermediate

Teruhiko Kadoyama
Simon Capper

photographs by
iStockphoto

A COMMUNICATIVE APPROACH TO THE TOEIC® L&R TEST
Book 2: Intermediate

LINGUAPORTA

リンガポルタのご案内

> リンガポルタ連動テキストをご購入の学生さんは、
> 「リンガポルタ」を無料でご利用いただけます!

　本テキストで学習していただく内容に準拠した問題を、オンライン学習システム「リンガポルタ」で学習していただくことができます。PCだけでなく、スマートフォンやタブレットでも学習できます。単語や文法、リスニング力などをよりしっかり身に付けていただくため、ぜひ積極的に活用してください。

　リンガポルタの利用にはアカウントとアクセスコードの登録が必要です。登録方法については下記ページにアクセスしてください。

https://www.seibido.co.jp/linguaporta/register.html

本テキスト「A COMMUNICATIVE APPROACH TO THE TOEIC® L&R TEST Book 2: Intermediate」の
アクセスコードは下記です。

7269-2047-1231-0365-0003-0074-H2J8-MT8R

・リンガポルタの学習機能（画像はサンプルです。また、すべてのテキストに以下の4つの機能が用意されているわけではありません）

● 多肢選択

● 空所補充（音声を使っての聞き取り問題も可能）

● 単語並びかえ（マウスや手で単語を移動）

● マッチング（マウスや手で単語を移動）

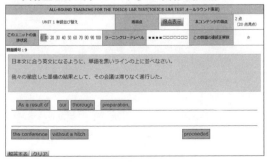

はしがき

　本書は、A Communicative Approach to the TOEIC® L&R Testシリーズの中級編であり、主に TOEIC® Listening and Reading Test（以下、TOEIC L&R テスト）でスコア 500〜600 を目指す方を対象としています。TOEIC L&R テスト対策のテキストは数多く出版されていますが、本書の特徴は、タイトルが示すように、コミュニケーションに焦点を当てたアプローチを採用した試験対策テキストであるという点です。具体的には、実践形式で練習問題を解いた後、問題で使われた対話や文書を活用して、パートナーと互いに英語で質問したり、質問に答えたりするコミュニケーション演習が本書には豊富に含まれています。試験対策の授業では予想問題を解くのが中心で、英語を話す機会がほとんどない場合もありますが、このテキストで学習することにより、単に TOEIC L&R テストのスコアアップだけではなく、英語のコミュニケーション能力を向上させることも可能となるでしょう。

　この他にも本書には次のような特徴があります。

　まず、各ユニットの最初にある Vocabulary のセクションでは、語彙の中でも特に派生語の増強に焦点を当てています。Part 5 の文法問題では正しい品詞を選ぶ問題が数多く出題されますが、派生語の知識を増やすことで、未知の単語であっても、語尾から意味や品詞を推測できるようになるでしょう。

　次に、各パートの問題を解くうえで知っておくべき重要項目を「解法のコツ」としてまとめており、効率的な学習が可能です。Part 3〜4 の図表問題や Part 6 の文挿入問題など、TOEIC L&R テストには特徴的な設問がいろいろありますが、解法のコツをマスターすることでそれらにも十分対応できるはずです。

　この他にも、本書は Web 英語学習システムの LINGUAPORTA（リンガポルタ）に対応していますので、パソコンやスマートフォンを使ったモバイル・ラーニングが可能です。

　TOEIC L&R テストは約 2 時間で 200問の問題を解かなければならず、スコアアップを図るにはやはり地道な英語学習が必要とされます。本書での学習が、皆さんの目標スコア獲得や英語コミュニケーション能力の涵養に役立てば、筆者としてこれ以上の喜びはありません。

　また、本書の刊行にあたっては、成美堂の佐野英一郎社長、そして編集部の工藤隆志氏、萩原美奈子氏に多大なご尽力を賜りました。衷心よりお礼申し上げます。

角山照彦
Simon Capper

Table of Contents

本書の構成と使い方

　本書は、オフィス、ショッピング、レストランなど、TOEIC L&R テストに頻出のテーマを取り上げた全 14 ユニットで構成されています。また、各ユニットは次のような構成になっています。

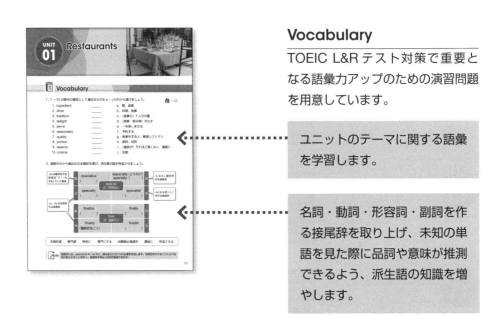

Vocabulary

TOEIC L&R テスト対策で重要となる語彙力アップのための演習問題を用意しています。

ユニットのテーマに関する語彙を学習します。

名詞・動詞・形容詞・副詞を作る接尾辞を取り上げ、未知の単語を見た際に品詞や意味が推測できるよう、派生語の知識を増やします。

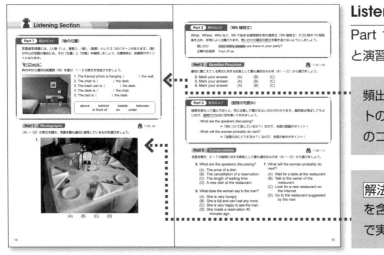

Listening Section

Part 1〜4 について、解法のコツと演習問題を用意しています。

頻出問題の解き方など、各パートの問題を解く際に必要な解法のコツを学習します。

解法のコツ で取り上げた内容を含む演習問題に取り組むことで実践力アップを目指します。

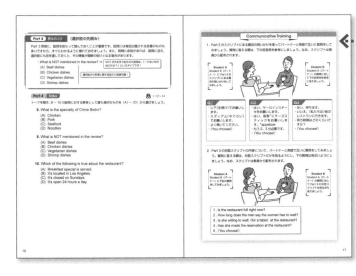

Communicative Training (Listening Section)

Part 2～4 で取り上げた応答や対話・トークを使ってパートナーと互いに英語で質問をしたり、質問に答えたりする演習です。

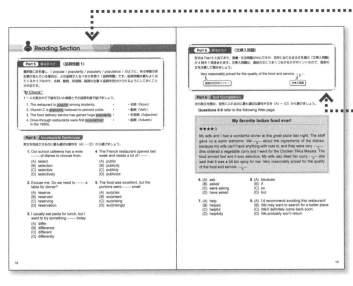

Reading Section

Part 5～7 について、解法のコツと演習問題を用意しています。

頻出問題の解き方など、各パートの問題を解く際に必要な解法のコツを学習します。

解法のコツ で取り上げた内容を含む演習問題に取り組むことで実践力アップを目指します。

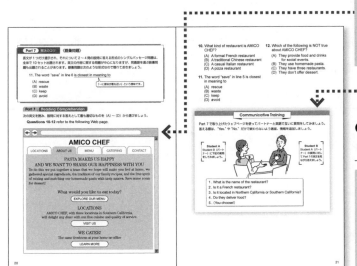

Communicative Training (Reading Section)

Part 7 で取り上げた文書を使ってパートナーと互いに英語で質問をしたり、質問に答えたりする演習です。

TOEIC® Listening and Reading Test について

　TOEIC® Listening and Reading Test（以下、TOEIC L&R テスト）は、アメリカの非営利団体 Educational Testing Service（ETS）によって開発されたテストです。TOEIC とは、**T**est **O**f **E**nglish for **I**nternational **C**ommunication の略称で、オフィスや日常生活における英語コミュニケーション能力を幅広く測定するテストですが、TOEIC L&R テストは、その中でも特に Listening と Reading の能力を測定するものです。（TOEIC テストには、TOEIC L&R テストの他にも TOEIC® Speaking & Writing Tests や TOEIC® Speaking Test があります。）

評価方法

　TOEIC L&R テストの結果は、合格や不合格ではなく、10 点から 990 点までのスコアで評価されます（リスニングセクション：5〜495 点、リーディングセクション：5〜495 点）。トータルスコアの基準は常に一定であり、英語能力に変化がない限りスコアも一定に保たれます。

問題形式

　リスニングセクション（約 45 分間・100問）とリーディングセクション（75 分間・100問）から構成されおり、約 2 時間で 200問の問題に解答しなければなりません。各セクションは、次の表が示すように、7 つのパートに分かれています。

セクション	パート	名称		形式	問題数
リスニングセクション	1	Photographs	写真描写問題	4 択	6 問
	2	Question-Response	応答問題	3 択	25 問
	3	Conversations	会話問題	4 択	39 問
	4	Talks	説明文問題	4 択	30 問
リーディングセクション	5	Incomplete Sentences	短文穴埋め問題	4 択	30 問
	6	Text Completion	長文穴埋め問題	4 択	16 問
	7	Reading Comprehension	読解問題	4 択	54 問

また、各パートの形式は以下のとおりです。

Part 1　Photographs

　1枚の写真について4つの短い説明文が1度だけ放送され、4つのうち写真を最も適切に描写しているものを選ぶ問題です。問題用紙には右のような写真のみで、説明文は印刷されていません。実際のテストでは6問出題され、解答時間は1問あたり約5秒です。

【問題例】

1.

Part 2　Question-Response

　1つの質問（または発言）と、3つの応答がそれぞれ1度だけ放送され、質問に対して最も適切な応答を3つの中から選ぶ問題です。問題用紙には質問も応答も印刷されていません。実際のテストでは25問出題され、解答時間は1問あたり約5秒です。

【問題例】

7. Mark your answer on your answer sheet.

Part 3　Conversations

　会話が1度だけ放送され、その後に設問が続きます。会話は印刷されていません。問題用紙の設問と4つの選択肢を読み、その中から最も適切なものを選ぶ問題です。実際のテストでは39問出題されます。解答時間は1問あたり約8秒ですが、図表問題のみ約12秒となっています。

【問題例】

32. Where does the woman work?

(A) At a restaurant
(B) At a hospital
(C) At a school
(D) At a post office

Part 4　Talks

　アナウンスや電話のメッセージなどの説明文（トーク）が1度だけ放送され、その後に設問が続きます。説明文は印刷されていません。問題用紙の設問と4つの選択肢を読み、その中から最も適切なものを選ぶ問題です。実際のテストでは30問出題されます。解答時間は1問あたり約8秒ですが、図表問題のみ約12秒となっています。

【問題例】

71. What is being advertised?

(A) A pharmacy
(B) A movie theater
(C) A fitness center
(D) A supermarket

Part 5 Incomplete Sentences

4つの選択肢の中から最も適切なものを選び、不完全な文を完成させる問題です。実際のテストでは30問出題されます。

【問題例】

101. Oysters are a ------- of this restaurant.

    (A) special
    (B) specialize
    (C) specially
    (D) specialty

Part 6 Text Completion

4つの選択肢の中から最も適切なものを選び、不完全な文書を完成させる問題です。実際のテストでは、1つの長文に対して4問ずつ問題があり、合計16問出題されます。

【問題例】

Online shopping is a fast-growing market in the U.S. In a survey ------- 131. in May last year, 40 percent of U.S.-based Internet users answered that they bought goods online several times a month.

131. (A) conduct
    (B) conducting
    (C) conducted
    (D) conducts

Part 7 Reading Comprehension

様々な形式の文書が提示され、それに関する設問と4つの選択肢を読んでその中から最も適切なものを選ぶ問題です。実際のテストでは、1つの文書に関する問題（シングルパッセージ問題）が29問、複数の文書に関する問題（ダブルパッセージ問題・トリプルパッセージ問題）が25問出題されます。

【問題例】

Dear all,
I hope this e-mail finds you all well.

147. The word "recommend" in paragraph 1, line 7, is closest in meaning to

    (A) suggest
    (B) deliver
    (C) provide
    (D) avoid

UNIT 01 Restaurants

Vocabulary

1. 1 ～ 10 の語句の意味として適切なものを a ～ j の中から選びましょう。 **1-02**

1. ingredient	＿＿＿＿	a．質、品質
2. diner	＿＿＿＿	b．料理、食事
3. tradition	＿＿＿＿	c．（食事の）1 人分の量
4. delight	＿＿＿＿	d．（食事・飲み物）を出す
5. serve	＿＿＿＿	e．～を楽しませる
6. reasonably	＿＿＿＿	f．予約する
7. quality	＿＿＿＿	g．食事をする人、軽食レストラン
8. portion	＿＿＿＿	h．原料、材料
9. reserve	＿＿＿＿	i．（値段が）それほど高くなく、適度に
10. cuisine	＿＿＿＿	j．伝統

2．語群の中から適切な日本語訳を選び、派生語の図を完成させましょう。

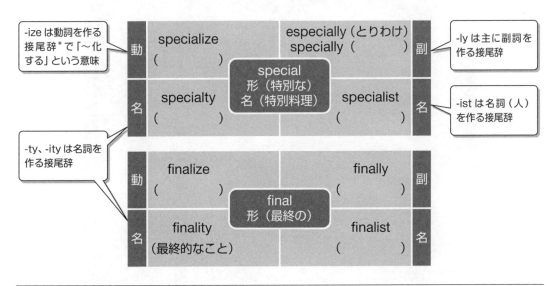

-ize は動詞を作る接尾辞＊で「～化する」という意味

動　specialize（　　　）

especially（とりわけ）
specially（　　　）　副

-ly は主に副詞を作る接尾辞

special
形（特別な）
名（特別料理）

名　specialty（　　　）

specialist（　　　）　名

-ist は名詞（人）を作る接尾辞

-ty、-ity は名詞を作る接尾辞

動　finalize（　　　）

finally（　　　）　副

final
形（最終の）

名　finality（最終的なこと）

finalist（　　　）　名

名物料理	専門家	特別に	専門にする	決勝戦出場選手	最後に	完成させる

 Note 接尾辞とは、specialist の -ist など、語の後ろに付けられる要素を指します。接尾辞を付けることにより品詞が変化することが多く、接尾辞を見ると品詞が推測できます。

Listening Section

Part 1 解法のコツ 〈物の位置〉

写真描写問題には、〈人物（1人、複数）〉、〈物〉、〈風景〉という3つのパターンがあります。〈物〉が中心の写真の場合には、その「位置」と「状態」を確認しましょう。位置関係は、前置詞がポイントになります。

☞ Check

枠の中から適切な前置詞（句）を選び、1〜5の英文を完成させましょう。

1. The framed photo is hanging (   ) the wall.
2. The chair is (   ) the desk.
3. The trash can is (   ) the desk.
4. The desk is (   ) the chair.
5. The bed is (   ) the desk.

above	behind	beside	between
	in front of	on	under

Part 1 Photographs

🎧 1-03, 04

（A）〜（D）の英文を聞き、写真を最も適切に描写しているものを選びましょう。

1.

(A)   (B)   (C)   (D)

Part 2 | 解法のコツ 〈Wh 疑問文〉

What、Where、Who など、Wh で始まる疑問詞を含む疑問文（Wh 疑問文）が 25 問中 10 問前後を占め、非常によく出題されます。問いかけの最初の部分を聞き逃さないようにしましょう。

問いかけ	How many people are there in your party?
正解の応答例	Four of us.

Part 2 | Question-Response

 1-05〜08

最初に聞こえてくる英文に対する応答として最も適切なものを（A）〜（C）から選びましょう。

2. Mark your answer.   (A)   (B)   (C)
3. Mark your answer.   (A)   (B)   (C)
4. Mark your answer.   (A)   (B)   (C)

Part 3 | 解法のコツ 〈設問の先読み〉

設問を前もって読んでおくと、何に注意して聞けばよいのかがわかります。選択肢は飛ばしてもよいので、設問だけは先に目を通しておきましょう。

・What are the speakers discussing?

⇒「何について話しているか？」なので、会話の話題がポイント！

・What will the woman probably do next?

⇒「会話の次にどうするか？」なので、会話の後半がポイント！

Part 3 | Conversations

 1-09〜11

会話を聞き、5 〜 7 の設問に対する解答として最も適切なものを（A）〜（D）から選びましょう。

5. What are the speakers discussing?

(A) The price of a dish
(B) The cancellation of a reservation
(C) The length of waiting time
(D) A new dish at the restaurant

6. What does the woman say to the man?

(A) She is very hungry.
(B) She is full and can't eat any more.
(C) She is very happy to see the man.
(D) She made a reservation 45 minutes ago.

7. What will the woman probably do next?

(A) Wait for a table at the restaurant
(B) Talk to the owner of the restaurant
(C) Look for a new restaurant on the Internet
(D) Go to the restaurant suggested by the man

Part 3 同様に、設問を前もって読んでおくことが重要です。設問には毎回出題される定番のものも多いですから、すぐにわかるように慣れておきましょう。また、時間に余裕があれば、設問に加え、選択肢にも目を通しておくと、その情報が理解の助けとなる場合があります。

・What is NOT mentioned in the review? ⇒ | NOT が大文字で記された設問は、「～でないものはどれか？」というタイプです！

(A) Beef dishes

(B) Chicken dishes

(C) Vegetarian dishes | 選択肢から料理に関する話だと推測可能！

(D) Shrimp dishes

Part 4 **Talks**   1-12～14

トークを聞き、8 ～ 10 の設問に対する解答として最も適切なものを（A）～（D）から選びましょう。

8. What is the specialty of China Bistro?

(A) Chicken
(B) Pork
(C) Seafood
(D) Noodles

9. What is NOT mentioned in the review?

(A) Beef dishes
(B) Chicken dishes
(C) Vegetarian dishes
(D) Shrimp dishes

10. Which of the following is true about the restaurant?

(A) Breakfast special is served.
(B) It's located in Los Angeles.
(C) It's closed on Sundays.
(D) It's open 24 hours a day.

Communicative Training

1. Part 2 のスクリプトにある最初の問いかけを使ってパートナーと英語で互いに質問をして みましょう。質問に答える際は、下の回答例を参考にしましょう。なお、スクリプトは教 員から配布されます。

Student A
Student B（パート ナー）に Part 2 の スクリプトにある最 初の問いかけをして みましょう。

Student B
Student A（パート ナー）の質問に対し て下の回答例を参考 に答えましょう。

Q2
- レア（生焼け）でお願いし ます。
- ミディアム（中ぐらい） でお願いします。
- よく焼いてください。
- (You choose!)

Q3
- はい、サーロインステー キをお願いします。
- はい、前菜*にチーズス ティックをお願いしま す。*appetizer
- もう2、3分必要です。
- (You choose!)

Q4
- はい、待ちます。
- いいえ、（私たちは）他の レストランに行きます。
- 待ち時間はどのくらいで すか？
- (You choose!)

2. Part 3 の対話スクリプトの内容について、パートナーと英語で互いに質問をしてみましょ う。質問に答える際は、対話スクリプトだけを見るようにし、下の質問は見ないようにし ましょう。なお、スクリプトは教員から配布されます。

Student A
Student B（パート ナー）に下記の質問 をしてみましょう。

Student B
Student A（パート ナー）の質問に対し て Part 3 の対話ス クリプトを見ながら 答えましょう。

1. Is the restaurant full right now?
2. How long does the man say the woman has to wait?
3. Is she willing to wait (for a table) at the restaurant?
4. Has she made the reservation at the restaurant?
5. (You choose!)

Part 5 解法のコツ 〈品詞問題 1〉

選択肢に目を通し、(popular / popularity / popularly / popularize) のように、ある単語の派生語が並んでいる場合は、どの品詞が入るべきかを問う「品詞問題」です。品詞問題は最もよく出てくるタイプなので、名詞、動詞、形容詞、副詞の主要 4 品詞を見分けられるようにしておくことが大切です。

☞ Check

1 ～ 4 の英文中で下線を引いた単語とその品詞を線で結びましょう。

1. The restaurant is popular among students. •
2. Vitamin C is popularly believed to prevent colds. •
3. The food delivery service has gained huge popularity. •
4. Drive-through restaurants were first popularized in the 1950s. •

- • 名詞（Noun）
- • 動詞（Verb）
- • 形容詞（Adjective）
- • 副詞（Adverb）

Part 5 Incomplete Sentences

英文を完成させるのに最も適切な語句を（A）～（D）から選びましょう。

1. Our school cafeteria has a wide ------- of dishes to choose from.

   (A) select
   (B) selection
   (C) selective
   (D) selectively

2. Excuse me. Do we need to ------- a table for dinner?

   (A) reserve
   (B) reserved
   (C) reserving
   (D) reservation

3. I usually eat pasta for lunch, but I want to try something ------- today.

   (A) differ
   (B) difference
   (C) different
   (D) differently

4. The French restaurant opened last week and needs a lot of ------- .

   (A) public
   (B) publicity
   (C) publicly
   (D) publicize

5. The food was excellent, but the portions were ------- small.

   (A) surprise
   (B) surprised
   (C) surprising
   (D) surprisingly

形式は Part 5 と似ており、語彙・文法問題が中心ですが、空所に当てはまる文を選ぶ「文挿入問題」が 4 問中 1 問含まれます。文挿入問題は、直前の文にうまくつながるかがポイントなので、直前の文を注意して読みましょう。

Very reasonably priced for the quality of the food and service. -------- .
9.

直前の文がポイント！

文挿入問題

Part 6　Text Completion

次の英文を読み、空所に入れるのに最も適切な語句や文を（A）〜（D）から選びましょう。

Questions 6-9 refer to the following Web page.

My favorite Indian food ever!

★★★★☆

My wife and I had a wonderful dinner at this great place last night. The staff gave us a warm welcome. We -------- about the ingredients of the dishes, 6. because my wife can't have anything with nuts in, and they were very --------- . 7. She ordered a vegetable curry and I went for the Chicken Tikka Masala. The food arrived fast and it was delicious. My wife also liked her curry, -------- she 8. said that it was a bit too spicy for her. Very reasonably priced for the quality of the food and service. -------- . 9.

6. (A) ask
   (B) asked
   (C) were asking
   (D) have asked

7. (A) help
   (B) helped
   (C) helpful
   (D) helpfully

8. (A) because
   (B) if
   (C) so
   (D) but

9. (A) I'd recommend avoiding this restaurant!
   (B) We may want to search for a better place.
   (C) We'll definitely come back soon.
   (D) We probably won't return.

長文が1つだけ提示され、それについて2～4問の設問に答える形式のシングルパッセージ問題は、全体で10セット出題されます。英文の内容に関する問題が中心になりますが、同義語を選ぶ語彙問題も出題されることがあります。語彙問題は次のような形式なので慣れておきましょう。

11. The word "save" in line 6 is closest in meaning to

(A) rescue
(B) waste
(C) keep
(D) avoid

「～に意味が最も近い」という意味です。

Part 7 **Reading Comprehension**

次の英文を読み、設問に対する答えとして最も適切なものを（A）～（D）から選びましょう。

Questions 10-12 refer to the following Web page.

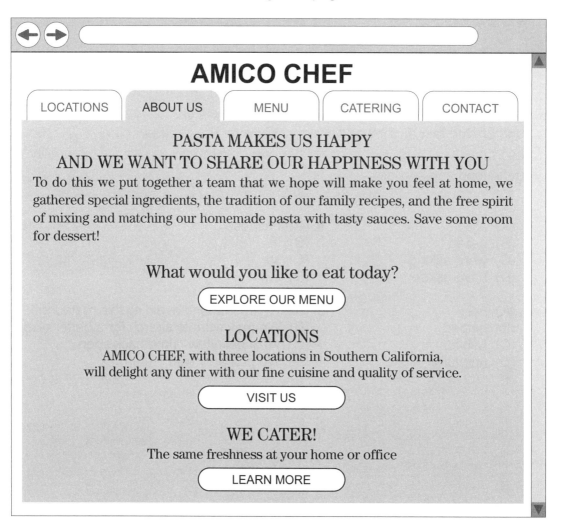

AMICO CHEF

| LOCATIONS | ABOUT US | MENU | CATERING | CONTACT |

PASTA MAKES US HAPPY
AND WE WANT TO SHARE OUR HAPPINESS WITH YOU

To do this we put together a team that we hope will make you feel at home, we gathered special ingredients, the tradition of our family recipes, and the free spirit of mixing and matching our homemade pasta with tasty sauces. Save some room for dessert!

What would you like to eat today?

(EXPLORE OUR MENU)

LOCATIONS
AMICO CHEF, with three locations in Southern California,
will delight any diner with our fine cuisine and quality of service.

(VISIT US)

WE CATER!
The same freshness at your home or office

(LEARN MORE)

10. What kind of restaurant is AMICO CHEF?

    (A) A formal French restaurant
    (B) A traditional Chinese restaurant
    (C) A casual Italian restaurant
    (D) A pizza restaurant

11. The word "save" in line 5 is closest in meaning to

    (A) rescue
    (B) waste
    (C) keep
    (D) avoid

12. Which of the following is NOT true about AMICO CHEF?

    (A) They provide food and drinks for social events.
    (B) They use homemade pasta.
    (C) They have three restaurants.
    (D) They don't offer dessert.

Communicative Training

Part 7 で取り上げたウェブページを使ってパートナーと英語で互いに質問をしてみましょう。
答える際は、"Yes." や "No." だけで終わらないよう適宜、情報を追加しましょう。

Student A
Student B（パートナー）に下記の質問をしてみましょう。

Student B
Student A（パートナー）の質問に対して Part 7 の英文を見ながら答えましょう。

1 . What is the name of the restaurant?

2 . Is it a French restaurant?

3 . Is it located in Northern California or Southern California?

4 . Do they deliver food?

5 . (You choose!)

主な接頭辞一覧

接頭辞とは、unable の un- など、語の先頭に付けられて、その語の意味あるいは機能を変える要素を指します。例えば、un- は通常、語の意味を逆にしますので、「(〜することが) できる」という意味の able に対して unable は「(〜することが) できない」という意味を表します。接尾辞同様、接頭辞の知識があると、未知の単語の意味をある程度推測できます。

接頭辞	意味	例
bi-	2 つの (two)	biweekly (隔週の) (< weekly)
dis-	〜でない (not)	disregard (無視する) (< regard)
in-, im-, il-, ir- ※ im- は p や m で始まる形容詞、ir- は r で始まる形容詞、il- は l で始まる形容詞の前につくことが多い。	〜でない (not)	incomplete (不完全な) (< complete) impossible (不可能な) (< possible) immature (未熟な) (< mature) illegal (不法の) (< legal) irregular (不規則な) (< regular)
mono-	1 つの (one)	monorail (モノレール) (< rail)
multi-	多くの (many)	multilingual (多数の言語を使える) (< lingual)
non-	〜でない (not)	nonprofit (非営利の) (< profit)
out-	外の (outside) 〜以上に (bigger, better, longer, etc.)	outpatient (外来患者) (< patient) outlive (〜より長生きする) (< live)
post-	後の (after)	post-tax (〈収入が〉税引き後の) (< tax)
pre-	前の (before)	pre-tax (〈収入が〉税引き前の) (< tax)
re-	再び (again)	reconsider (再考する) (< consider)
semi-	半分 (half)	semifinal (準決勝の) (< final)
un-	〜でない (not) 元に戻して (back)	unkind (不親切な) (< kind) undo (元に戻す) (< do)

pre- 前の (before)
prewar (戦前の)

post- 後の (after)
postwar (戦後の)

war
戦争

UNIT 02 Offices

 Vocabulary

1. 1 ～ 10 の語句の意味として適切なものを a ～ j の中から選びましょう。　🎧 1-15

1. branch	＿＿＿＿	a．平等
2. register	＿＿＿＿	b．（仕事などを）担当して
3. notify	＿＿＿＿	c．不便な、都合の悪い
4. maintenance	＿＿＿＿	d．取引先、顧客
5. inconvenient	＿＿＿＿	e．組織
6. currently	＿＿＿＿	f．支店、営業所
7. organization	＿＿＿＿	g．通知する
8. client	＿＿＿＿	h．（建物などの）維持、保守
9. equality	＿＿＿＿	i．登録する
10. in charge	＿＿＿＿	j．現在は、今のところ

2. 語群の中から適切な単語を選び、「会議」、「会社」、「同僚」、「部署」に関する関連語の表を完成させましょう。

会議	会社	同僚	部署
meeting			

✔meeting　　department　　company　　coworker　　firm

division　　colleague　　conference　　corporation

Listening Section

Part 1 解法のコツ 〈人物（1人）の描写〉

〈人物（1人、複数）〉、〈物〉、〈風景〉という3つのパターンのうち、人物が1人だけ写っている写真の場合、その人の「動作」と「状態」を確認しましょう。特に put on（動作）と wear（状態）の違いを問う問題は注意が必要です。

The woman is wearing a mask.
（女性はマスクをしています）[状態]

The woman is putting on a mask.
（女性はマスクをつけようとしています）[動作]

Part 1 **Photographs**   CD 1-16, 17

（A）～（D）の英文を聞き、写真を最も適切に描写しているものを選びましょう。

1.

(A)   (B)   (C)   (D)

Yes か No かで答えることが可能な疑問文（Yes / No 疑問文）も Wh 疑問文と並んでよく出題されます。「よくわかりません」のように、応答は必ずしも Yes / No で始まるとは限らないので注意しましょう。

| 問いかけ | Is Patricia in charge of this sales campaign? |
| 正解の応答例 | Sorry. I have no idea. |

Part 2　Question-Response　　　　　　　　　　　　　🎧 1-18〜21

最初に聞こえてくる英文に対する応答として最も適切なものを（A）〜（C）から選びましょう。

2. Mark your answer.　　　(A)　　　(B)　　　(C)
3. Mark your answer.　　　(A)　　　(B)　　　(C)
4. Mark your answer.　　　(A)　　　(B)　　　(C)

Part 3　解法のコツ　〈定番の設問〉

会話の話題や場所、話し手の職業など、毎回出題される定番の設問があるので、設問を見たらすぐにわかるように慣れておきましょう。　　　| most likely で「おそらく」という意味 |

・What are the speakers talking about?　⇒会話の話題がポイント！
・Where most likely are the speakers?　⇒会話が行われている場所がポイント！
・What does the woman suggest?　⇒女性が提案している内容がポイント！
・What does the woman suggest the man do?　⇒女性が男性に提案している内容がポイント！

Part 3　Conversations　　　　　　　　　　　　　🎧 1-22〜24

会話を聞き、5〜7 の設問に対する解答として最も適切なものを（A）〜（D）から選びましょう。

5. What are the speakers talking about?

(A) Their client
(B) Their deadline
(C) Their appointment
(D) Their boss

6. What does the woman suggest?

(A) They should meet at another time.
(B) They should have the meeting now.
(C) She would cancel her appointment.
(D) She would accompany him.

7. What will the man probably do this afternoon?

(A) Hold a meeting with the woman
(B) Pay a visit to his client
(C) Go to the woman's office
(D) Rearrange his office

Part 4　解法のコツ　〈Talk の種類〉

1 人の話し手によるトークには、電話のメッセージやラジオ放送、店内放送など、様々な種類が登場します。実際の問題ではトークが始まる前に次のような指示文が読まれるので、そこでトークの種類がわかります。トークの種類によって内容をある程度推測できるので、慣れておきましょう。

> トークの種類が示されます。

Questions 71-73 refer to the following telephone message.

> 「〜に関するものだ」という意味です。

Check

1 〜 5 の英文中で下線を引いた語句とその日本語訳を線で結びましょう。

1. Questions XXX-XXX refer to the following advertisement. 　•　　•ツアー情報
2. Questions XXX-XXX refer to the following excerpt from a meeting. •　　•放送
3. Questions XXX-XXX refer to the following broadcast. 　•　　•会議の抜粋
4. Questions XXX-XXX refer to the following tour information. 　•　　•お知らせ
5. Questions XXX-XXX refer to the following announcement. 　•　　•広告

Part 4　Talks

1-25〜27

トークを聞き、8 〜 10 の設問に対する解答として最も適切なものを（A）〜（D）から選びましょう。

8. What type of business does the speaker most likely work for?

(A) A dry cleaner's
(B) A sports collectibles store
(C) A used game store
(D) A sports gym

9. What is mentioned about the store?

(A) It is closed for refurbishment.
(B) It is closed for the holidays.
(C) It is closed every Monday.
(D) It will reopen soon.

10. What should you do if you want to leave a message?

(A) Press 0
(B) Press 1
(C) Press 2
(D) Press 3

26

Communicative Training

1. Part 2 のスクリプトにある最初の問いかけを使ってパートナーと英語で互いに質問をしてみましょう。質問に答える際は、下の回答例を参考にしましょう。なお、スクリプトは教員から配布されます。

Student A
Student B（パートナー）に Part 2 のスクリプトにある最初の問いかけをしてみましょう。

Student B
Student A（パートナー）の質問に対して下の回答例を参考に答えましょう。

Q2
・はい、私が担当です。 ・いいえ、ビルが担当です。 ・いいえ、私は担当ではありません。 ・(You choose!)

Q3
・ええ、そうです。ありがとうございます。 ・はい、（私はそれを）ずっと探していました。 ・いいえ、私は販売報告書を探しているのです。 ・(You choose!)

Q4
・もちろんです。（私たちは）もっと人が必要です。 ・いいえ、（私たちは）これ以上雇う必要はありません。 ・そうですね、（私には）よくわかりません。 ・(You choose!)

2. Part 3 の対話スクリプトの内容について、パートナーと英語で互いに質問をしてみましょう。質問に答える際は、対話スクリプトだけを見るようにし、下の質問は見ないようにしましょう。なお、スクリプトは教員から配布されます。

Student A
Student B（パートナー）に下記の質問をしてみましょう。

Student B
Student A（パートナー）の質問に対して Part 3 の対話スクリプトを見ながら答えましょう。

1. What does the man want to do with the meeting?
2. What time was today's meeting originally scheduled to start?
3. What does the man have to do this afternoon?
4. What time is the rearranged meeting scheduled to start tomorrow?
5. (You choose!)

 # Reading Section

Part 5 解法のコツ 〈動詞の形問題 **1**〉

選択肢に目を通し、(make / has made / is making / made) のように、ある動詞の活用形が並んでいる場合は、動詞の形を問う問題です。動詞の形を問う問題は、時制を問うものと、態（受動態かそれとも能動態か）を問うものの 2 種類に分けられますが、時制の場合、時を表す語句（now や last night など）が決め手になります。

☞Check゛

下線部に注意しながら、1 〜 4 の英文中のカッコ内から正しい語句を選び○で囲みましょう。

1. Luke (makes / is making) a presentation <u>right now</u>.
2. We (have been working / are working) on the project <u>for five weeks</u>.
3. Tim <u>usually</u> (leaves / is leaving) the office at five.
4. I (have attended / attended) that workshop <u>two days ago</u>.

Part 5 **Incomplete Sentences**

英文を完成させるのに最も適切な語句を（A）〜（D）から選びましょう。

1. Oh, there you are! Mr. Mason ------- for you since this morning.

(A) waits
(B) waited
(C) is waiting
(D) has been waiting

2. The Chicago branch of our company ------- exactly one year ago today.

(A) opens
(B) has opened
(C) opened
(D) was opening

3. Until a month ago, I usually ------- lunch at the company cafeteria.

(A) eat
(B) ate
(C) have eaten
(D) am eating

4. Currently, Mr. Hawthorne ------- for a new assistant.

(A) looks
(B) looked
(C) is looking
(D) had been looking

5. If you don't attend tomorrow's meeting, you ------- a chance to talk with the president.

(A) miss
(B) have missed
(C) will miss
(D) going to miss

Part 6 では、手紙や e メール、メモ、広告、通知、指示など、様々な種類の文書が登場します。文書の種類によって書式上の特徴があるので、文書の種類を即座に掴むことが重要です。また、実際の問題では次のような指示文が記載されるので、そこで文書の種類がわかります。

文書の種類が示されます。

Questions 131-134 refer to the following Web page.

☞ Check

1 〜 5 の英文中で下線を引いた単語とその日本語訳を線で結びましょう。

1. Questions XXX-XXX refer to the following advertisement.　•
2. Questions XXX-XXX refer to the following brochure.　•
3. Questions XXX-XXX refer to the following article.　•
4. Questions XXX-XXX refer to the following notice.　•
5. Questions XXX-XXX refer to the following instructions.　•

• 記事
• 通知
• パンフレット
• 指示
• 広告

Part 6 **Text Completion**

次の英文を読み、空所に入れるのに最も適切な語句や文を（A）〜（D）から選びましょう。

Questions 6-9 refer to the following notice.

Grand Plaza Office Building
Notice to all tenants — Fire Alarm Test

Please note that on Friday, March 13, the Grand Plaza maintenance office ------- a test of the fire alarm system. This is part of our regular maintenance
    6.
work and is necessary to comply ------- city safety regulations. The alarm will
    7.
sound several times over a 30-minute period, from 1:00 P.M. to 1:30 P.M.
Please disregard all alarms and do not evacuate the building at this time. We
will notify you upon ------- of the test.
    8.

In the unlikely event of a genuine emergency, each office will be notified. ------- .
    9.

6. (A) conducted
   (B) is conducted
   (C) have conducted
   (D) will be conducting

7. (A) with
   (B) to
   (C) for
   (D) by

8. (A) complete
   (B) completely
   (C) completion
   (D) completed

9. (A) We are looking forward to March 13.
   (B) We received your feedback with much
       appreciation.
   (C) The last maintenance work turned out to
       be a great success.
   (D) We apologize for any inconvenience.

Part 7 で出題される文書の中でも e メールは頻出書式の 1 つです。次の書式例で書式の特徴に慣れておきましょう。

eメールの書式例

From:
To:
Date:
Subject:
Attachment:

■ヘッダー

送信者、受信者、日付、件名、添付物が記されます。件名（Subject）は概要理解のヒントになるので必ず確認しましょう。

Dear Mr. Smith,

■本文

最初に、宛先（＝受信者）が記されます。Dear Mr. Smith のように、Dear から始まることが多いですが、親しい間柄の場合、Hi, Rick のようになることもあります。

次に、用件が述べられ、ここが問題の中心になるので、じっくり読みましょう。結びは、(Yours) Sincerely のほか、(Best) Regards などもよく使われます。

Sincerely,

Ian Freely
Manager
Human Resources
ABC Bank

■フッター

送信者の氏名、所属（役職、部署、会社名）が記されます。

Part 7 Reading Comprehension

次の英文を読み、設問に対する答えとして最も適切なものを（A）〜（D）から選びましょう。

Questions 10-13 refer to the following e-mail.

To:	All departments
From:	ifreely@abcbank.com (Human Resources)
Date:	September 22
Subject:	Gender Equality Workshop

Dear colleagues,

Organizations such as ours require management to practice approaches that effectively promote gender equality and women's leadership. Therefore, we will be holding a workshop on gender equality. The workshop will not only help us to see gender equality from a fresh perspective, it will also strengthen interpersonal skills for improved communication and networking.

Please be advised that all employees in senior management positions will be required to attend one of the workshops, to be held on the second Friday of each month (October, November and December) from 10:00-12:00, in the Ferguson Suite. Failure to attend on one of these dates will result in you having to attend an off-site workshop at your own expense.

Please follow this link to register for your preferred workshop date. For any further information, please contact Human Resources.

Sincerely,

Ian Freely
Manager
Human Resources

10. What is the purpose of the e-mail?

   (A) To gather ideas for future workshops
   (B) To collect data on gender equality
   (C) To extend an invitation to a charity event
   (D) To announce a training session

11. What is indicated about the workshop?

   (A) It will be held in the Ferguson Suite.
   (B) It will be held only in the evening.
   (C) It will be held weekly from October through December.
   (D) All full-time employees have to attend it.

12. The word "expense" in paragraph 2, line 5, is closest in meaning to

   (A) risk
   (B) pace
   (C) cost
   (D) convenience

13. What is the receiver of the e-mail asked to do?

   (A) Inform Human Resources of his or her decision
   (B) Register for his or her preferred workshop date
   (C) Submit his or her ideas on gender equality
   (D) Plan and conduct future workshops

Communicative Training

Part 7 で取り上げた e メールを使ってパートナーと英語で互いに質問をしてみましょう。答える際は、"Yes." や "No." だけで終わらないよう適宜、情報を追加しましょう。

Student A
Student B（パートナー）に下記の質問をしてみましょう。

Student B
Student A（パートナー）の質問に対して Part 7 の英文を見ながら答えましょう。

1. When was this e-mail sent?

2. Who wrote it?

3. Who is Mr. Freely?

4. What is the workshop about?

5. Where will it be held?

6. Will it be held in the morning or in the afternoon?

7. (You choose!)

UNIT 03 Daily Life

📖 Vocabulary

1. 1～10の語句の意味として適切なものをa～jの中から選びましょう。　💿 1-28

1. account	＿＿＿＿	a.	混乱させる、戸惑わせる
2. forecast	＿＿＿＿	b.	気前の良い
3. retail	＿＿＿＿	c.	信頼できる
4. confuse	＿＿＿＿	d.	（苦情など）を申し立てる
5. clothing	＿＿＿＿	e.	生活用品、必需品
6. generous	＿＿＿＿	f.	取引先、得意先
7. supplies	＿＿＿＿	g.	形式的行為
8. lodge	＿＿＿＿	h.	予測する
9. formality	＿＿＿＿	i.	衣類
10. reliable	＿＿＿＿	j.	小売り

2. 語群の中から適切な日本語訳を選び、派生語の図を完成させましょう。

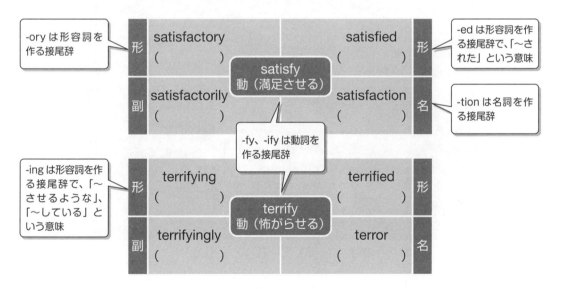

満足のいくように　満足　満足できる　満足した　恐ろしいほど　おびえた　恐怖　恐ろしい

33

Part 1 解法のコツ 〈人物（2人）の描写〉

2人の人物が写っている写真の場合、「向かい合っている」や「並んでいる」のように、位置関係を確認しましょう。

They're facing each other.
（彼らは向かい合っています）

They're walking side by side.
（彼らは並んで歩いています）

They're looking in the same direction.
（彼らは同じ方向を見ています）

Part 1 Photographs

1-29, 30

（A）〜（D）の英文を聞き、写真を最も適切に描写しているものを選びましょう。

1.

(A)　　(B)　　(C)　　(D)

最初の問いかけに出てきた単語が入った選択肢は不正解である場合がほとんどです。問いかけが理解できなかった受験者は、選択肢の中に問いかけに使われていた単語が聞こえるとついその選択肢を選ぶ傾向があるため、出題者は意図的に不正解の選択肢として用意しているのです。

問いかけ	How was the field trip?
不正解の応答例	We go on a field trip every year.
正解の応答例	Not bad, I guess.

Part 2 **Question-Response** 1-31～34

最初に聞こえてくる英文に対する応答として最も適切なものを（A）～（C）から選びましょう。

2. Mark your answer. (A) (B) (C)
3. Mark your answer. (A) (B) (C)
4. Mark your answer. (A) (B) (C)

Part 3 解法のコツ 〈理由を問う設問〉

理由を尋ねる設問では、"Why did the man arrive late?" のように why で始まるものが定番です。会話の中の発言を取り上げ、その発言をした理由を問うタイプもあるので慣れておきましょう。また、選択肢は "He missed his train." のような文タイプか、"To surprise the woman" のような不定詞のタイプとなります。不定詞タイプの選択肢は短いものが多いので、できるだけ会話を聞く前に選択肢まで見ておくようにしましょう。会話のヒントが得られます。

・Why does the man say, "Who's the lucky girl"?

(A) To ask who got married   会話の中に出てくる発言です。
(B) To ask who had a baby
(C) To ask who got a job   不定詞タイプの選択肢は短いものが多いです。
(D) To ask who entered university

Part 3 **Conversations** 1-35～37

会話を聞き、5 ～ 7 の設問に対する解答として最も適切なものを（A）～（D）から選びましょう。

5. What are the speakers talking about?

(A) Their parents
(B) Their children
(C) Their job
(D) Their college days

6. Why does the man say, "Who's the lucky girl"?

(A) To ask who got married
(B) To ask who had a baby
(C) To ask who got a job
(D) To ask who entered university

7. Who most likely is Jenny?

(A) A school teacher
(B) A high school student
(C) A college student
(D) A graduate student

オリエンテーションやツアーの案内では、下記のような基本的な流れがあります。予定が順番に話されるので、時刻や場所を聞き漏らさないに注意しましょう。

1. 呼びかけ	Hello, my name is Brad and I'll be your museum guide this afternoon.
	⇒ツアーの場所は博物館！
2. 予定	We'll start by visiting a special exhibition of Italian Renaissance drawings for an hour until 3 P.M.
	⇒最初は特別展を鑑賞予定！
3. 注意事項	Please remember, you're not allowed to take photos of the art works.
	⇒写真撮影は禁止！
4. 結び	OK, let's begin. Please follow me.
	⇒ツアーの開始！

Part 4　Talks

🎧 1-38〜40

トークを聞き、8 〜 10 の設問に対する解答として最も適切なものを（A）〜（D）から選びましょう。

8. Where does the tour most likely take place?

(A) At a fruit farm
(B) At a garden
(C) At a farmer's market
(D) At a tea factory

9. What will listeners do at the end of the tour?

(A) Receive a gift
(B) Make some herbal tea
(C) Enjoy some refreshments
(D) Learn about tropical plants

10. What will listeners find in the brochure?

(A) A coupon
(B) Directions to the gift shop
(C) A list of souvenirs
(D) A tea bag

Communicative Training

1. Part 2のスクリプトにある最初の問いかけを使ってパートナーと英語で互いに質問をしてみましょう。質問に答える際は、下の回答例を参考にしましょう。なお、スクリプトは教員から配布されます。

<table>
<tr><td>Student A
Student B（パートナー）にPart 2のスクリプトにある最初の問いかけをしてみましょう。</td><td>Student B
Student A（パートナー）の質問に対して下の回答例を参考に答えましょう。</td></tr>
</table>

Q2
- 彼女は素晴らしい上司です。
- 彼女のことはまだよく知りません。
- そうですね、あなたはどう思っているのですか？
- (You choose!)

Q3
- はい、オーストラリアとカナダに行ったことがあります。
- いいえ、海外に行ったことは一度もありません。
- いいえ、ありません。しかし、いつかスペインに行ってみたいです。
- (You choose!)

Q4
- 実は、転職する*ことを考えています。
   * change jobs
- ごめんなさい。今はそれについて話したくありません。
- ジョンのことが心配です。
- (You choose!)

---

2. Part 3の対話スクリプトの内容について、パートナーと英語で互いに質問をしてみましょう。質問に答える際は、対話スクリプトだけを見るようにし、下の質問は見ないようにしましょう。なお、スクリプトは教員から配布されます。

<table>
<tr><td>Student A
Student B（パートナー）に下記の質問をしてみましょう。</td><td>Student B
Student A（パートナー）の質問に対してPart 3の対話スクリプトを見ながら答えましょう。</td></tr>
</table>

1. Who got married, Danny or Jenny?
2. Who is Lizzy?
3. What does Jenny do?
4. Is Jenny in graduate school?
5. (You choose!)

Reading Section

Part 5 解法のコツ 〈品詞問題2〉

品詞問題で問われる品詞は、主に名詞、動詞、形容詞、副詞の4つです。形容詞と副詞は共に「説明を加える」役割を果たすため区別が難しいですが、確実に見分けられるようにしましょう。形容詞と副詞を見分けるポイントは次のとおりです。

形容詞	名詞に説明を加えます。 ex.) We had a **wonderful** time . / The dinner was **great**.
副　詞	名詞以外（動詞、形容詞、副詞など）に説明を加えます。 ex.) This software is **wonderfully** easy to use.

☞Check

網掛けの語に注意して1〜4の英文中のカッコ内から正しい語を選び○で囲みましょう。

1. I (complete / completely) forgot that it's my mother's birthday today.
2. None of the solutions was entirely (satisfactory / satisfactorily).
3. The fact that something is cheap doesn't (necessary / necessarily) mean it's of low quality.
4. Rick looked at her with a (surprised / surprisedly) expression on his face.

Part 5 Incomplete Sentences

英文を完成させるのに最も適切な語句を（A）〜（D）から選びましょう。

1. Mark was ------- warned not to work so hard, but he didn't care.

   (A) repeat
   (B) repeatedly
   (C) repetitive
   (D) repeated

2. Alma felt hurt and ------- when her husband left her.

   (A) confusing
   (B) confusingly
   (C) confuse
   (D) confused

3. The government has lodged a ------- protest against the arrest of the foreign reporters.

   (A) formally
   (B) formal
   (C) formality
   (D) formalize

4. The ------- of Mr. and Mrs. Mellon made the museum project possible.

   (A) generous
   (B) generously
   (C) generosity
   (D) most generous

5. This Web site helps you find what you want faster and more ------- .

   (A) reliable
   (B) rely
   (C) reliability
   (D) reliably

文脈の理解が必要となる問題では、「したがって」や「しかし」のように、2 つの文をつなぐ副詞（句）を選ばせるものが登場します。これらの副詞（句）は、読解の際に非常に重要ですから確実にマスターしておきましょう。

☞ Check

語群から適切な語句を書き入れ、表を完成させましょう。

結果（したがって、それゆえ）	逆接（しかし、それどころか）	情報追加（さらに、しかも）
	however	

語群

in addition	✓however	therefore	moreover
besides	on the contrary	as a result	thus

Part 6 Text Completion

次の英文を読み、空所に入れるのに最も適切な語句や文を（A）〜（D）から選びましょう。

Questions 6-9 refer to the following article.

(June 10) Back-to-school sales at U.S. department stores are expected to jump about 15% from last year, as parents ------- a lot of money on clothing, supplies and electronics for the new academic year, when most kids return ------- classrooms, an industry report showed on Friday.
6.
7.

Sales at department stores during this back-to-school season, which runs mid-July through early-September, ------- to rise 15.7% from a year earlier, according to Ultradata Inc. ------- .
8.
9.

6. (A) save
(B) spend
(C) make
(D) borrow

7. (A) at
(B) in
(C) from
(D) to

8. (A) are forecast
(B) forecast
(C) forecasts
(D) forecasting

9. (A) Therefore, sales at department stores dropped sharply last year.
(B) However, back-to-school sales will start next week.
(C) Total retail sales are projected to rise 5.5%.
(D) As a result, children have to prepare for another school year.

Part 6 〜 7 では手紙やメモ、広告、通知など、様々な種類の文書が登場しますが、Part 7 特有な形式としてオンラインチャットが挙げられます。次のような指示文が記載され、1 〜 2 問出題されます。

> Questions 147-148 refer to the following text-message chain.
> Questions 161-164 refer to the following online discussion.

また、チャット特有の問題として、「〇時〇分に、●●さんは〜と書いていますが、どういう意味でしょうか？」のように、チャットで使われた表現を引用し、話者の意図を尋ねるものがあります。

> ■ At 12:39, what does Ms. Taylor most likely mean when she writes, "Of course, I won't"?

引用された表現の文字どおりの意味ではなく、チャットのやりとりの中でどのように使われているかをよく考えて答えるようにしましょう。

Part 7　Reading Comprehension

次の英文を読み、設問に対する答えとして最も適切なものを（A）〜（D）から選びましょう。

Questions 10-12 refer to the following message chain.

PAUL GREEN [12:30]
Hi, I'm in the parking lot. Where are you?

RACHEL TAYLOR [12:32]
In the cafeteria with Liz. We agreed to meet at one o'clock, right?

PAUL GREEN [12:35]
That's right. But the traffic's heavy today, so we should leave earlier. Mr. Miller won't be happy if we're late for the meeting. Anyway, he's the president of our biggest account. Can you come a little earlier?

RACHEL TAYLOR [12:36]
Well, I've just started eating, but all right. How about in 10 minutes?

PAUL GREEN [12:37]
That's fine, but please hurry. And don't forget to bring the presentation slides we worked on.

RACHEL TAYLOR [12:39]
Of course, I won't. We spent too much time working on them to forget them now.

PAUL GREEN [12:40]
Great.

RACHEL TAYLOR [12:46]
I'm on my way. See you soon.

10. Why is Mr. Green waiting for Ms. Taylor?

   (A) To have lunch with her
   (B) To work on the presentation slides
   (C) To drive with her to a meeting
   (D) To open a bank account

11. Who most likely is Mr. Miller?

   (A) The head of a company
   (B) Mr. Green's colleague
   (C) Mr. Green's boss
   (D) An accountant

12. At 12:39, what does Ms. Taylor most likely mean when she writes, "Of course, I won't"?

   (A) She won't hurry up.
   (B) She will arrive in time.
   (C) She will never forget the hours they worked on the slides.
   (D) She'll remember to bring the slides.

Communicative Training

Part 7 で取り上げたチャットを使ってパートナーと英語で互いに質問をしてみましょう。答える際は、"Yes." や "No." だけで終わらないよう適宜、情報を追加しましょう。

Student A
Student B（パートナー）に下記の質問をしてみましょう。

Student B
Student A（パートナー）の質問に対して Part 7 の英文を見ながら答えましょう。

1. Where is Paul?
2. Is Rachel in the parking lot?
3. What time did they originally agree to meet?
4. Why does he want to leave earlier?
5. Who is Mr. Miller?
6. What does Paul ask Rachel to bring with her?
7. (You choose!)

UNIT 04 Personnel

AB CD Vocabulary

1. 1 〜 10 の語句の意味として適切なものを a 〜 j の中から選びましょう。　CD 1-41

1. budget	_____	a．議題
2. resign	_____	b．転勤させる
3. qualification	_____	c．申し込む
4. agenda	_____	d．候補者
5. experienced	_____	e．辞任する
6. apply	_____	f．〜を見直す、〜を再検討する
7. review	_____	g．経験豊富な
8. transfer	_____	h．履歴書
9. candidate	_____	i．資格、必要条件
10. résumé	_____	j．予算

2. 語群の中から適切な日本語訳を選び、派生語の図を完成させましょう。

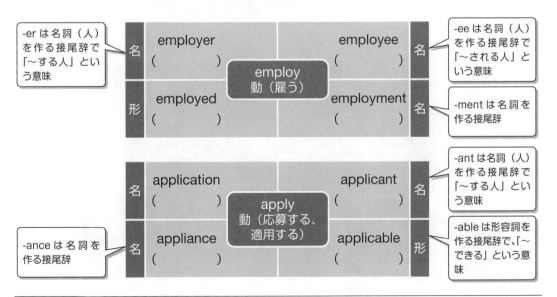

-er は名詞（人）を作る接尾辞で「〜する人」という意味

-ee は名詞（人）を作る接尾辞で「〜される人」という意味

-ment は名詞を作る接尾辞

名 employer（　　　）

名 employee（　　　）

employ 動（雇う）

形 employed（　　　）

名 employment（　　　）

-ant は名詞（人）を作る接尾辞で「〜する人」という意味

-able は形容詞を作る接尾辞で、「〜できる」という意味

-ance は名詞を作る接尾辞

名 application（　　　）

名 applicant（　　　）

apply 動（応募する、適用する）

名 appliance（　　　）

形 applicable（　　　）

雇用　雇用された　従業員　雇用主　適用できる　応募者　電気器具　申し込み・適用

Listening Section

Part 1 解法のコツ 〈人物（3人以上）の描写 1〉

3人以上の人物が写っている写真の場合、「彼らは全員〜している」のように、共通点を描写するものと、「1人の男性が〜している」のように、人物の中で目立つ人物について描写するタイプとに分かれます。They'reで始まる文が聞こえた場合は、全員の共通点を描写しているかどうか確認しましょう。ただし、写真から全員の職業などが明らかな場合は、workers や travelers のような具体的な単語が主語として使われることもあります。

📖 **Check**

1〜6の語句とその日本語訳とを線で結びましょう。

1. cashier ・ ・建設作業員
2. server ・ ・歩行者
3. diner ・ ・配管工
4. construction worker ・ ・レジ係
5. pedestrian ・ ・食事客
6. plumber ・ ・給仕係

Part 1 **Photographs** 🎧 1-42, 43

（A）〜（D）の英文を聞き、写真を最も適切に描写しているものを選びましょう。

1.

(A) (B) (C) (D)

Part 2 解法のコツ 〈否定疑問文〉

Yes / No 疑問文の中には、"Don't you like it?" のように文頭が否定語で始まる否定疑問文があります。日本語だと「はい、好きではありません」と答えられますが、英語の場合は、通常の疑問文であろうと否定疑問文であろうと、肯定するなら Yes、否定するなら No と答えると覚えておきましょう。

問いかけ	Didn't you apply for the job?
不正解の応答例	Yes, I wasn't interested. / No, I did.
正解の応答例	Of course, I did.

Part 2 Question-Response

 1-44〜47

最初に聞こえてくる英文に対する応答として最も適切なものを（A）〜（C）から選びましょう。

2. Mark your answer.　　　(A)　　　(B)　　　(C)
3. Mark your answer.　　　(A)　　　(B)　　　(C)
4. Mark your answer.　　　(A)　　　(B)　　　(C)

Part 3 解法のコツ 〈時を問う設問〉

時を尋ねる設問では、"When does the woman want to see the man?" のように when で始まるものが定番ですが、この他にも how often や how soon など様々な疑問詞を使って尋ねられることがありますので慣れておきましょう。

・How often does the train run?	⇒「どのくらいの間隔」で頻度がポイント！
・How long have they been waiting?	⇒「どのくらい」で時間の長さがポイント！
・How soon does the concert begin?	⇒「どのくらいすぐ」で開始時期がポイント！
・How long ago did the woman order?	⇒「どのくらい前」で過去の時期がポイント！

Part 3 Conversations

1-48〜50

会話を聞き、5 〜 7 の設問に対する解答として最も適切なものを（A）〜（D）から選びましょう。

5. Why did Julia miss the meeting?

  (A) She had a traffic accident.
  (B) She was on vacation.
  (C) She was sick.
  (D) She arrived too late.

6. What does the man want to show the woman?

  (A) A sales report
  (B) A budget report
  (C) A personnel record
  (D) A new contract

7. When does the woman want to see the man?

  (A) At 3 o'clock today
  (B) At 5 o'clock today
  (C) At 10 o'clock tomorrow
  (D) At 11 o'clock tomorrow

社内アナウンスには、下記のような基本的な流れがあるので、情報がどのような順序で出てくるか予測することができます。慣れておきましょう。

1. 挨拶	Good afternoon, everyone.
2. 目的	Just before we start today's meeting, I'd like to take this opportunity to introduce Ms. Heather Graham. ⇒人物の紹介
3. 詳細	She's visiting from our Boston office, where she's been a senior sales representative. She'll be taking over as sales manager when Martin retires at the end of this month. ⇒人物に関する詳細の説明
4. 追加情報	Ms. Graham will take some time to meet each of you after the meeting. ⇒面会予定の連絡
5. 結び	Thank you.

Part 4　Talks

 1-51〜53

トークを聞き、8 〜 10 の設問に対する解答として最も適切なものを（A）〜（D）から選びましょう。

8. What is the main purpose of this talk?

(A) To introduce a new branch manager
(B) To revise the orientation program for new hires
(C) To announce job openings
(D) To announce staff members to be transferred to Seattle

9. What is indicated about Seattle?

(A) The company's headquarters will be moved there.
(B) A branch office will be opened there.
(C) The speaker will be transferred there.
(D) A new factory will be built there.

10. What will most likely be discussed next?

(A) New travel procedures
(B) An acquisition of a start-up company
(C) Sales in the Seattle office
(D) A program for new employees

Communicative Training

1. Part 2 のスクリプトにある最初の問いかけを使ってパートナーと英語で互いに質問をして みましょう。質問に答える際は、下の回答例を参考にしましょう。なお、スクリプトは教 員から配布されます。

Student A
Student B（パート ナー）に Part 2 の スクリプトにある最 初の問いかけをして みましょう。

Student B
Student A（パート ナー）の質問に対し て下の回答例を参考 に答えましょう。

Q2
・（はい、）していません。 もっと考える時間が必要 です。
・（はい、）していません。 それには興味がありませ ん。
・（いいえ、）先週応募しま した。
・（You choose!）

Q3
・（いいえ、）それにはとて も興味があります。
・（はい、）それにはまった く興味ありません。
・あなたはそれに興味ある のですか？
・（You choose!）

Q4
・彼がオフィスにいなかっ たからです。
・言おうとしたのですが、 彼は聞いてくれませんで した。
・そうですね、そうする必 要はないと思ったのです。
・（You choose!）

2. Part 3 の対話スクリプトの内容について、パートナーと英語で互いに質問をしてみましょ う。質問に答える際は、対話スクリプトだけを見るようにし、下の質問は見ないようにし ましょう。なお、スクリプトは教員から配布されます。

Student A
Student B（パート ナー）に下記の質問 をしてみましょう。

Student B
Student A（パート ナー）の質問に対し て Part 3 の対話ス クリプトを見ながら 答えましょう。

1. Was Julia absent from the meeting because she was sick?
2. What does the woman have to do with Julia?
3. What does the man want to show the woman?
4. Where will the man and woman meet at 10 o'clock tomorrow?
5. (You choose!)

Part 5　解法のコツ　〈品詞問題 3〉

命令文などを除き、通常、英文には主語と（述語）動詞があります。品詞問題のうち名詞と動詞は、主語と（述語）動詞、そして目的語（動作の対象）という英文の基本要素を把握することが見分けるポイントです。

名　詞	人や物事などの名称を表し、主語や目的語となります。 ex.) Further **resignations** are expected. / We haven't received his **resignation** yet.
動　詞	主語の動作や状態を示します。 ex.) He **resigned** as president after eight years.

☞Check

1～4の英文中のカッコ内から正しい語を選び○で囲みましょう。

1. If I can't get (promote / a promotion) soon, I'll look for another job.
2. Who would you (recommend / recommendation) for this job?
3. (Attend / Attendance) at the dinner is by invitation only.
4. You must submit your (apply / application) before July 1.

Part 5　Incomplete Sentences

英文を完成させるのに最も適切な語句を（A）～（D）から選びましょう。

1. A team of legal ------- were employed to work on the case.

- (A) specialists
- (B) special
- (C) specialized
- (D) specialize

2. Whether we ------- or fail depends on good luck and hard work.

- (A) success
- (B) successful
- (C) successfully
- (D) succeed

3. We want our ------- to behave in a calm and professional manner.

- (A) employ
- (B) employees
- (C) employed
- (D) employment

4. Pedro wanted to improve his English so he could ------- as a translator.

- (A) qualify
- (B) qualified
- (C) qualifier
- (D) qualification

5. I don't expect any ------- from my friends on the tennis court.

- (A) favorable
- (B) favored
- (C) favors
- (D) favorably

文挿入問題を除いて、Part 6 の問題形式は Part 5 と似ていますが、Part 5 と同様に空所を含む一文だけで解答可能な問題の他に、前後の文脈の理解が必要な問題も含まれています。こうした問題の場合、空所を含む文だけでは解答できないため、必ず直前・直後の文を読み文脈を確認しましょう。

🖝 Check

下線を引いた文に注意して、空所に当てはまる単語を（A）～（D）の中から選びましょう。

<u>We received your comments with much appreciation.</u> ----1.--- feedback is used to help us improve our services.

> この文だけでは正解にはたどり着けません。

1. (A) Their
   (B) Its
   (C) His
   (D) Your

Part 6　Text Completion

次の英文を読み、空所に入れるのに最も適切な語句や文を（A）～（D）から選びましょう。

Questions 6-9 refer to the following Web page.

Applying Online

On May 1, 2022, the Transportation Authority of Clay County launched an online employment application ----6.--- better serves job applicants.

All applicants, ----7.--- previous applicants, will be required to create a new account and fill out an online employment application when ----8.--- for a position.

If you experience any problems, please contact Human Resources at 123-456-7890. You are welcome to apply at our Administration Building. ----9.--- .

---

6. (A) this
   (B) that
   (C) who
   (D) whose

7. (A) with
   (B) for
   (C) upon
   (D) including

8. (A) applying
   (B) apply
   (C) applied
   (D) to apply

9. (A) Unfortunately, we will not be offering you the position.
   (B) We received your application with much appreciation.
   (C) We have a computer kiosk available for applicants to apply in our lobby.
   (D) We currently have no job vacancies.

指定の文に対して最も適した挿入箇所を選ぶ「文挿入問題」は、前後の文脈を見極めなければならず、他の問題に比べて難易度が高いです。そのため、解答するのを最後に回すのも1つの手です。また、文挿入問題は次のような形式なので、慣れておきましょう。

10. In which of the positions marked [1], [2], [3], and [4] does the following sentence best belong?

"Prior to that, I worked for three years in the billing department of a local gas company."

この文が入る適切な位置を [1]〜[4] から選びます。

(A) [1]

(B) [2]

(C) [3]

(D) [4]

Part 7　Reading Comprehension

次の英文を読み、設問に対する答えとして最も適切なものを（A）〜（D）から選びましょう。

Questions 10-13 refer to the following letter.

July 17, 2023

Ms. Amanda Baker
Human Resources Director
Right Aid Corporation
125 Union Square
New Hope, PA 18938

Dear Ms. Baker,

I am interested in applying for the position as an accountant you advertised in the Sunday edition of the *Times Tribune*. — [1] —. I am enclosing my résumé and two letters of reference. I have all the qualifications for the job. I recently received my master's degree in Accounting from Pennsylvania State University. Before I entered graduate school, I worked for five years as a bookkeeper for a toy company. — [2] —. I also have experience using the computer software your ad mentioned. — [3] —.

I hope you will consider me as a candidate for the position. — [4] —. I look forward to hearing from you.

Sincerely yours,

Craig Newton

Craig Newton

10. Why did Mr. Newton write the letter?

    (A) To advertise a position
    (B) To apply to a graduate school
    (C) To ask for a letter of reference
    (D) To reply to an advertisement for an opening

11. Where did Mr. Newton work?

    (A) At a toy company
    (B) At a graduate school
    (C) At an advertising company
    (D) At a newspaper company

12. What is indicated about Mr. Newton?

    (A) He only has a bachelor's degree.
    (B) He and Ms. Baker used to be colleagues.
    (C) He wishes to work at Right Aid Corporation.
    (D) He placed an advertisement in the Sunday edition of the *Times Tribune*.

13. In which of the positions marked [1], [2], [3], and [4] does the following sentence best belong?
"Prior to that, I worked for three years in the billing department of a local gas company."

    (A) [1]
    (B) [2]
    (C) [3]
    (D) [4]

Communicative Training

Part 7 で取り上げた手紙を使ってパートナーと英語で互いに質問をしてみましょう。答える際は、"Yes." や "No." だけで終わらないよう適宜、情報を追加しましょう。

Student A
Student B（パートナー）に下記の質問をしてみましょう。

Student B
Student A（パートナー）の質問に対して Part 7 の英文を見ながら答えましょう。

1. What company does Ms. Baker work for?
2. What department does she belong to?
3. What position is Mr. Newton interested in applying for?
4. What does he enclose with the letter?
5. What degree did he get from the university?
6. What did he do before he entered graduate school?
7. (You choose!)

本テキストで取り上げている接尾辞一覧 1

　接尾辞とは、specialist の -ist など、語の後ろに付けられる要素を指します。接尾辞を付けることにより品詞が変化することが多く、接尾辞を見ると品詞が推測できます。例えば exist（存在する）という動詞の後ろに -ence が付くことにより existence（存在）という名詞になります。次の表を使って本テキストで取り上げている名詞を作る接尾辞を確認しましょう。

名詞を作る接尾辞

接尾辞	意味		例
-ant	人	～する人	applicant（応募者）（< apply）
-ee		～される人	interviewee（面接を受ける人、受験者）（< interview）
-er		～する人	interviewer（面接官）（< interview）
-ian		～する人	magician（手品師）（< magic）
-ist		～な人、～する人	specialist（専門家）（< special）
-or		～する人	educator（教育者）（< educate）
-ance	こと、状態		compliance（遵守）（< comply）
-ence			existence（存在）（< exist）
-ency			emergency（緊急事態）（< emerge）
-ion, -sion, -tion			invention（発明）（< invent）
-ity, -ty			security（安全）（< secure）
-ment			excitement（興奮）（< excite）
-ness			politeness（礼儀正しさ）（< polite）

-er（～する人）
employer（雇用主）

employ
雇用する

-ee（～される人）
employee（従業員）

UNIT 05 Shopping

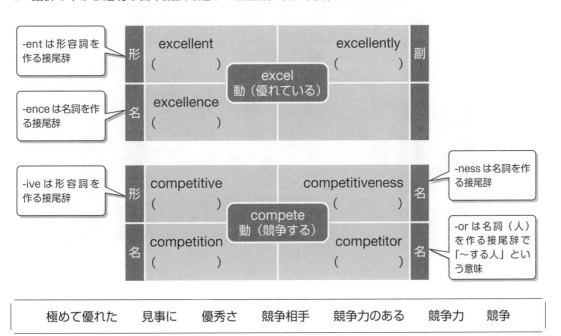Vocabulary

1. 1 〜 10 の語句の意味として適切なものを a 〜 j の中から選びましょう。　　🎧 1-54

1. voucher	_____	a．謝罪
2. purchase	_____	b．（商品・サービスの）引換券
3. refund	_____	c．送り状、明細付き請求書
4. item	_____	d．（特別な）出来事、行事、機会
5. occasion	_____	e．返金
6. apology	_____	f．商品、品物
7. invoice	_____	g．無料の
8. charge	_____	h．購入（品）、購入する
9. replace	_____	i．（代金、支払いなど）を請求する
10. complimentary	_____	j．〜を取り換える

2. 語群の中から適切な日本語訳を選び、派生語の図を完成させましょう。

-ent は形容詞を作る接尾辞

-ence は名詞を作る接尾辞

形　excellent（　　　）　　　副　excellently（　　　）

名　excellence（　　　）

excel 動（優れている）

-ive は形容詞を作る接尾辞

-ness は名詞を作る接尾辞

-or は名詞（人）を作る接尾辞で「〜する人」という意味

形　competitive（　　　）　　　名　competitiveness（　　　）

名　competition（　　　）　　　名　competitor（　　　）

compete 動（競争する）

極めて優れた	見事に	優秀さ	競争相手	競争力のある	競争力	競争

53

Listening Section

Part 1 解法のコツ 〈風景の描写〉

風景写真の場合、まずどのような場所かを把握しましょう。また、人物写真の場合と違い、選択肢の主語がすべて異なることも多いので、写真と照合しながら聞き取りましょう。また、人がいないことを示す unoccupied や empty などの表現にも慣れておきましょう。

The desks are unoccupied.
（机は空いています）

The road is lined with trees.
（道路には木が立ち並んでいます）

The street is empty.
（通りには人通りがありません）

Part 1 **Photographs**

1-55, 56

（A）〜（D）の英文を聞き、写真を最も適切に描写しているものを選びましょう。

1.

(A)　　(B)　　(C)　　(D)

Part 2 解法のコツ 〈選択疑問文〉

"A or B?" という形式の選択疑問文は Yes / No では答えられないので、Yes / No で始まる選択肢は不正解となります。基本的には A か B のどちらかを選ぶ応答が正解になりますが、「どちらでもありません」や「どちらでも良いです」のような応答が正解になることもあります。

問いかけ	Is this store closed on Monday or Tuesday?
正解の応答例	Neither. It's closed on Wednesday.
問いかけ	Which do you prefer, tea or coffee?
正解の応答例	Either is fine with me.

Part 2 / Question-Response

CD 1-57〜60

最初に聞こえてくる英文に対する応答として最も適切なものを（A）〜（C）から選びましょう。

2. Mark your answer.　　(A)　　　(B)　　　(C)
3. Mark your answer.　　(A)　　　(B)　　　(C)
4. Mark your answer.　　(A)　　　(B)　　　(C)

Part 3 解法のコツ 〈次の行動を問う設問〉

"What will the man probably do next?" のように、会話の後に話し手がどのような行動をするかを問う設問は頻出問題の 1 つです。3 つある設問のうち最後の設問として登場することが多く、会話における最後の発言がポイントになるので、注意して聞き取りましょう。

・What will the man probably do next?
・What does the man ask the woman to do?
・What does the man say he will do?
・What is the man asked to do?

> 会話の最後で何と言っているかに注意しましょう！

Part 3 / Conversations

CD 1-61〜63

会話を聞き、5 〜 7 の設問に対する解答として最も適切なものを（A）〜（D）から選びましょう。

5. What is wrong with the pants?

(A) They are too short.
(B) They are too long.
(C) They are too formal.
(D) They are too casual.

6. What does the woman say about the jacket?

(A) It is a bit too large.
(B) It is very expensive.
(C) It won't last long.
(D) The quality is good.

7. What will the man probably do next?

(A) Go to the cashier
(B) Go to a different store
(C) Try on another jacket
(D) Buy a dress for the woman

Part 4 解法のコツ 〈店内アナウンス〉

店内アナウンスには、下記のような基本的な流れがあるので、情報がどのような順序で出てくるか予測することができます。慣れておきましょう。

1. 呼びかけ	Can I have your attention, please?	
2. 目的	It's 9:45, and we will be closing in 15 minutes. Please bring all your purchases to one of the check-out stands.	
	⇒閉店時間のお知らせ	
3. 追加情報、注意事項		
	Those already in a check-out line by 10 will be served, but the front doors will be locked at that time.	
	⇒閉店時間での正面ドア閉鎖の案内	
4. 結び	Thank you for shopping with us tonight, and have a good night.	
	⇒謝辞	

Part 4 Talks

 1-64〜66

トークを聞き、8 〜 10 の設問に対する解答として最も適切なものを (A) 〜 (D) から選びましょう。

8. What type of store is this?

(A) A clothing store
(B) A grocery store
(C) A bakery
(D) A candy store

9. What is indicated about the offer on the chips?

(A) The price has been reduced by 10 percent.
(B) They have been marked down by 65 percent.
(C) You can get a free sample if you buy one packet.
(D) You can get two packets of the chips for the price of one.

10. How long is the offer?

(A) One day
(B) Two days
(C) Three days
(D) One week

Communicative Training

1. Part 2 のスクリプトにある最初の問いかけを使ってパートナーと英語で互いに質問をして
   みましょう。質問に答える際は、下の回答例を参考にしましょう。なお、スクリプトは教
   員から配布されます。

Student A
Student B（パート
ナー）に Part 2 の
スクリプトにある最
初の問いかけをして
みましょう。

Student B
Student A（パート
ナー）の質問に対し
て下の回答例を参考
に答えましょう。

Q2
- そうですね、私は黒いほ
  うが好きです。
- 黒いほうですね。あなた
  に本当によく似合いま
  すよ。
- どちらもとてもいいで
  すよ。
- (You choose!)

Q3
- はい、フォーマルなスー
  ツを探しています。
- はい、セール中のノート
  パソコン*はあります
  か？   *laptop
- いいえ、ただ見ているだ
  けです。ありがとう。
- (You choose!)

Q4
- 自分用です。
- 母への贈り物です。
- 贈り物です。贈り物用に
  包装して*もらえます
  か？   *gift-wrap
- (You choose!)

2. Part 3 の対話スクリプトの内容について、パートナーと英語で互いに質問をしてみましょ
   う。質問に答える際は、対話スクリプトだけを見るようにし、下の質問は見ないようにし
   ましょう。なお、スクリプトは教員から配布されます。

Student A
Student B（パート
ナー）に下記の質問
をしてみましょう。

Student B
Student A（パート
ナー）の質問に対し
て Part 3 の対話ス
クリプトを見ながら
答えましょう。

1. What does the woman say about the jacket?
2. According to the man, what is wrong with the pants?
3. Does he think the suit is too formal?
4. Is he going to buy the suit?
5. (You choose!)

Part 5 解法のコツ 〈動詞の形問題2〉

動詞の形を問う問題は時制を問うものが中心ですが、態(受動態かそれとも能動態か)を問うものも含まれます。受動態かそれとも能動態かを問うだけであれば2択ですが、実際の問題では選択肢が4つありますので、惑わされないようにしましょう。

能動態	「〜は…する」のように、何かに働きかける意味を表します。 ex.) Fred **cleans** the store every morning.
受動態	「〜は…される/されている」のように、何らかの動作を受ける意味を表します。 ex.) The store **is cleaned** every morning.

☞**Check**

1～4の英文中のカッコ内から正しい語句を選び○で囲みましょう。

1. Your order (expects / is expected) to arrive today.

2. All the employees must (be worn / wear) uniforms at this store.

3. We (hired / were hired) five new staff members last month.

4. My credit card (stole / was stolen) while I was shopping.

Part 5 **Incomplete Sentences**

英文を完成させるのに最も適切な語句を(A)～(D)から選びましょう。

1. Charlie had to ------- the microwave to the store because it was defective.

(A) returning
(B) returned
(C) return
(D) be returned

2. Our shop ------- in September next year after a complete remodeling.

(A) reopen
(B) reopening
(C) has been reopened
(D) will reopen

3. Please keep in mind that tickets must ------- at least two weeks in advance.

(A) purchase
(B) purchased
(C) purchasing
(D) be purchased

4. New Jersey is one of the few states that do not ------- sales tax on clothing.

    (A) charge
    (B) be charged
    (C) have charged
    (D) charging

5. To celebrate Eastwood Mall's 20th anniversary, our food court and restaurants ------- you a special 10% meal discount today.

    (A) are offered
    (B) are offering
    (C) offering
    (D) offers

Part 6 解法のコツ 〈つなぎ言葉 2〉

2 つの文をつなぐ副詞（句）では、すでに取り上げた「結果」、「逆接」、「情報追加」に加えて、「例示」、「順序」、「条件」などもよく登場するので、これらについても確認しておきましょう。

☞ Check

語群から適切な語句を書き入れ、表を完成させましょう。

順序（まず、それから、最後に）	例示（例えば）	条件（さもなければ）
first		

語群

finally	for example	otherwise	✓first	next	for instance	then

次の英文を読み、空所に入れるのに最も適切な語句や文を（A）～（D）から選びましょう。

Questions 6-9 refer to the following letter.

Johnson Jewelers
3200 21st Street Suite 500
Bakersfield, CA 93301

June 8

Dear Ms. Miller,

Johnson Jewelers would like to thank you for your purchase. The diamond accessories ------- bought from us will make you stand out on any occasion.
6.
Please let us know if you need any post-purchase services. ------- .
7.

We have enclosed a gift voucher with this letter offering a 10% discount for your next purchase. The voucher is ------- for the next 6 months.
8.

Once again, thank you for choosing Johnson Jewelers for your purchase. We look forward to ------- you again.
9.

Sincerely,

Melissa Johnson
Manager, Johnson Jewelers

---

6. (A) we
(B) you
(C) it
(D) your

7. (A) Finally, you are one of our valued customers.
(B) First, we hope you enjoy showing off the jewelry.
(C) Do visit our store soon in order to make use of this discount.
(D) For example, you can get free polishing and repair services from us.

8. (A) valid
(B) worthless
(C) timely
(D) costly

9. (A) see
(B) saw
(C) seeing
(D) having seen

Part 7 の後半では、複数の文書が 1 セットになった問題が計 5 題出題されます。その内訳は次のようになっています。

名称	形式	出題数
ダブルパッセージ問題	2 つの文書を読み 5 つの設問に答える	2 題
トリプルパッセージ問題	3 つの文書を読み 5 つの設問に答える	3 題

問題の指示文は次のようになっており、文書の形式がわかります。

　　Questions 176-180 refer to the following e-mail and schedule.

　　　　　　　　　　　　　　　　　　　⇒ダブルパッセージ問題の例

　　Questions 196-200 refer to the following Web page and e-mails.

　　　　　　　　　　　　　　　　　　　⇒トリプルパッセージ問題の例

いずれも難易度が高く、5 つの設問の中には必ず複数の文書の情報を組み合わせないと解けない問題が含まれています。ただし、それ以外の問題はシングルパッセージ問題と変わらないので、そうした問題から先に取り組むと良いでしょう。複数の文書の中で特定の文書に関する設問には、According to the e-mail（e メールによれば）や In the e-mail（e メールの中で）のような指示が含まれることもあります。

　　14. According to the second e-mail, what does Mr. Duncan offer to provide?

　　　　複数文書のうち、2 番目の e メールだけを読めば解ける問題です。

次の英文を読み、設問に対する答えとして最も適切なものを（A）～（D）から選びましょう。

Questions 10-14 refer to the following e-mails.

From:	Hilary Holmes <h.holmes@pmail.com>
To:	Customer Service <customer.service@angeldinnerware.com>
Date:	May 26
Subject:	Order #1066890

Dear Sir or Madam,

I recently placed an online order with Angel Dinnerware for a Mercer Dinnerware set (order #1066890). The order arrived this morning, and I found out that there is a crack in one of the five salad plates that are included in the set. I'm attaching the picture of the cracked plate to this e-mail.

In the past, I have ordered several times from your company and I received the shipments in perfect condition, so I'm surprised and disappointed with this order. I'd like you to replace the cracked plate with a new one.

Please contact me at <h.holmes@pmail.com> if you need any further information. I hope this matter will be taken care of as soon as possible.

Sincerely,

Hilary Holmes

From:	Customer Service <customer.service@angeldinnerware.com>
To:	Hilary Holmes <h.holmes@pmail.com>
Date:	May 27
Subject:	Re: Order #1066890

Dear Ms. Holmes,

I sincerely apologize for the trouble you had with your recent order. Could I ask you to send the damaged item back to us? We will replace it with a new one immediately once we have received it from you. Please find attached a label that you can print out and use for the return of the item. This label gives you free shipping.

As a token of our apology, we would like to offer you a 20 percent discount on your next purchase. Please use coupon code XYZ256696 to receive the discount.

Thank you in advance for your kind cooperation, and we do hope to do business with you again.

Sincerely yours,

Kenneth Duncan
Customer Service
Angel Dinnerware, Ltd.

10. What is the purpose of the first e-mail?

(A) To offer a replacement
(B) To request a discount
(C) To report a problem
(D) To place an order

11. What does Ms. Holmes send with her e-mail?

(A) A picture
(B) An invoice
(C) A product return form
(D) An order sheet

12. What does Mr. Duncan ask Ms. Holmes to send?

(A) A set of plates
(B) A plate
(C) A salad bowl
(D) A crack

13. In the second e-mail, the word "token" in paragraph 2, line 1, is closest in meaning to

(A) rule
(B) example
(C) basis
(D) sign

14. According to the second e-mail, what does Mr. Duncan offer to provide?

(A) A full refund
(B) A replacement of a complete set
(C) A label for complimentary shipping
(D) A latest product

Communicative Training

Part 7 で取り上げた e メールを使ってパートナーと英語で互いに質問をしてみましょう。答える際は、"Yes." や "No." だけで終わらないよう適宜、情報を追加しましょう。

Student A
Student B (パートナー) に下記の質問をしてみましょう。

Student B
Student A (パートナー) の質問に対して Part 7 の英文を見ながら答えましょう。

1. Did Ms. Holmes send the e-mail on May 27?
2. What did she recently order from Angel Dinnerware?
3. According to Ms. Holmes, what is the problem?
4. Is this the first time she's placed an order with Angel Dinnerware?
5. What does she want for the cracked plate?
6. What does Mr. Duncan ask her to do?
7. (You choose!)

接尾辞の中には、語の後ろに付いて動詞や形容詞、副詞を作るものもあります。例えば origin（起源）という名詞の後ろに -ate がつくことにより originate（始まる）という動詞になります。次の表を使って本テキストで取り上げている動詞、形容詞、副詞を作る接尾辞を確認しましょう。

動詞を作る接尾辞

接尾辞	意味	例
-ate*	～にする	originate（始まる）（< origin）
-en		widen（～を広くする）（< wide）
-fy, -ify		simplify（単純化する）（< simple）
-ize		specialize（専門にする）（< special）

＊必ずしも動詞とは限らず、fortunate（幸運な）のように形容詞を作る場合もあるので注意が必要。

形容詞を作る接尾辞

接尾辞	意味	例
-able	～できる	imaginable（想像できる）（< imagine）
-al	～の	additional（追加の）（< addition）
-ed	～された	satisfied（満足した）（< satisfy）
-ent	～な	excellent（極めて優れた）（< excel）
-ful	～に満ちた	careful（注意深い）（< care）
-ic	～に関する	atomic（原子の、原子力の）（< atom）
-ical	～に関する	historical（歴史の）（< history）
-ing	～させるような、～している	exciting（興奮させるような）（< excite）
-ive	～な	active（活動的な）（< act）
-less	～のない	careless（不注意な）（< care）
-ory	～な	satisfactory（満足できる）（< satisfy）
-ous	～な	dangerous（危険な）（< danger）

副詞を作る接尾辞

接尾辞	意味	例
-ly*	～なように	specially（特別に）（< special）

＊必ずしも副詞とは限らず、weekly（毎週の）のように形容詞を作る場合もあるので注意が必要。

-ing（～させるような）
boring（退屈な）

-ed（～された）
bored（退屈した）

bore
退屈させる

UNIT 06 Finances

AB/CD Vocabulary

1. 1 ～ 10 の語句の意味として適切なものを a ～ j の中から選びましょう。 🎧 1-67

1. purse	＿＿＿	a. 指揮、監督
2. raise	＿＿＿	b. 年金
3. contribute	＿＿＿	c. 退職
4. administrative	＿＿＿	d. 昇給
5. withdraw	＿＿＿	e. （専門家との）相談、協議
6. retirement	＿＿＿	f. 管理（上）の、経営（上）の
7. supervision	＿＿＿	g. 財布、ハンドバック
8. pension	＿＿＿	h. （預金）を引き出す
9. investment	＿＿＿	i. 投資
10. consultation	＿＿＿	j. 貢献する

2. 語群の中から適切な日本語訳を選び、派生語の図を完成させましょう。

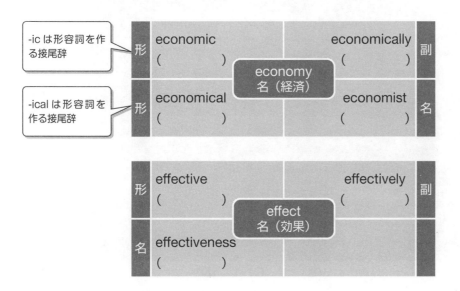

-ic は形容詞を作る接尾辞	形 economic (　　　)	economically (　　　) 副
-ical は形容詞を作る接尾辞	形 economical (　　　)	economist (　　　) 名

economy 名（経済）

形 effective (　　　)	effectively (　　　) 副
名 effectiveness (　　　)	

effect 名（効果）

経済学者	経済的に	経済的な・節約の	経済の	効果的に	効果的な	有効性

Listening Section

Part 1 解法のコツ 〈現在進行形〉

人物写真の場合、その人の「動作」と「状態」を描写するのに現在進行形が多く使われます。〈am / is / are+ 動詞の ing 形〉の部分を聞き逃さないようにしましょう。

☞ Check

下の写真の描写として最も適切な英文を 1 ～ 4 の中から選びましょう。

1. Someone is taking out his wallet from his pocket.
2. Someone is counting money with his hands.
3. Someone is grabbing money with his hands.
4. Someone is holding a lot of banknotes in his hand.

Part 1 **Photographs** 1-68, 69

（A）～（D）の英文を聞き、写真を最も適切に描写しているものを選びましょう。

1.

(A)　　(B)　　(C)　　(D)

Part 2 解法のコツ 〈付加疑問文〉

「〜ですよね？」のように、相手に同意を求めたり、念を押したりする疑問文（付加疑問文）の答え方は、基本的に Yes / No 疑問文と同じです。

問いかけ	You got a raise, didn't you?
正解の応答例	Yes, I'm so happy.

Part 2 Question-Response 1-70〜73

最初に聞こえてくる英文に対する応答として最も適切なものを（A）〜（C）から選びましょう。

2. Mark your answer. (A) (B) (C)
3. Mark your answer. (A) (B) (C)
4. Mark your answer. (A) (B) (C)

Part 3 解法のコツ 〈図表問題 1〉

図表を見ながら解答する問題では、設問を先に読む際に図表にも目を通しておきましょう。3 つの設問のうち図表に関するものは基本的に 1 つで、"Look at the graphic." という指示文が設問の始めに書かれています。

図表を見て答える問題を示しています。

Today's Schedule	
10:00	Client Consultation
11:00	
Noon	
1:00	Conference Call
3:00	
4:00	Staff Meeting
5:00	

7. Look at the graphic. When will the speakers most likely meet Tony?
   (A) 11:00
   (B) 3:00
   (C) 4:00
   (D) 5:00

Part 3 Conversations 1-74〜76

会話を聞き、5 〜 7 の設問に対する解答として最も適切なものを（A）〜（D）から選びましょう。

Today's Schedule	
10:00	Client Consultation
11:00	
Noon	
1:00	Conference Call
3:00	
4:00	Staff Meeting
5:00	

6. What does the woman need?
   (A) Some advice about investment
   (B) A pension
   (C) A new job
   (D) A fund-raising party

7. Look at the graphic. When will the speakers most likely meet Tony?
   (A) 11:00
   (B) 3:00
   (C) 4:00
   (D) 5:00

5. Who is Tony?
   (A) A career adviser
   (B) A health care professional
   (C) A pension fund adviser
   (D) A professional photographer

設問は、「何についてのメッセージですか？」のような概要に関する設問と、「締め切りはいつですか？」のような細かい内容に関する設問の2つに分かれます。また、多くの場合、3つの設問のうち第1問は概要に関する設問で、第2～3問が細かい内容に関する設問となっています。その場合、設問はトークの流れに沿って出題されるので、第2問はトークの前半、第3問は後半に関連していると考えてよいでしょう。

Part 4 **Talks**

 1-77～79

トークを聞き、8～10の設問に対する解答として最も適切なものを（A）～（D）から選びましょう。

8. What is this talk about?

(A) A loan program
(B) Retirement planning support
(C) A financial problem
(D) A change in retirement age system

9. What is indicated about the program?

(A) It is conducted twice a year.
(B) It has received excellent feedback from financial advisers.
(C) It started 10 years ago.
(D) It has been conducted for five years.

10. When does the reservation have to be made?

(A) By June 13
(B) By the end of June
(C) By July 5
(D) By the end of July

Communicative Training

1. Part 2 のスクリプトにある最初の問いかけを使ってパートナーと英語で互いに質問をして みましょう。質問に答える際は、下の回答例を参考にしましょう。なお、スクリプトは教 員から配布されます。

Student A
Student B（パート ナー）に Part 2 の スクリプトにある最 初の問いかけをして みましょう。

Student B
Student A（パート ナー）の質問に対し て下の回答例を参考 に答えましょう。

Q2
・はい、すでに支払いま した。
・いいえ、まだです。
・今払います。
・（You choose!）

Q3
・はい、ビルが昨日そう言 いました。
・いいえ、そうは思いませ んよ。
・えっ？ それは本当なの ですか？
・（You choose!）

Q4
・はい、それをとても楽し みにしています。
・いいえ、そうは思いませ んよ。
・本当ですか？ 誰がそう 言ったのですか？
・（You choose!）

---

2. Part 3 の対話スクリプトの内容について、パートナーと英語で互いに質問をしてみましょ う。質問に答える際は、対話スクリプトだけを見るようにし、下の質問は見ないようにし ましょう。なお、スクリプトは教員から配布されます。

Student A
Student B（パート ナー）に下記の質問 をしてみましょう。

Student B
Student A（パート ナー）の質問に対し て Part 3 の対話ス クリプトを見ながら 答えましょう。

1. Who is a pension fund adviser, Keith or Tony?
2. What does the woman need some advice about?
3. Will the man give her Tony's contact details?
4. When is he meeting Tony today?
5. （You choose!）

Reading Section

Part 5 解法のコツ 〈語彙問題〉

選択肢に目を通し、(little / light / short / tight) のように、同じ品詞の単語が並んでいる場合は、語彙の知識を問う「語彙問題」です。語彙問題も品詞問題と同様によく出題されますが、① borrow と lend、rent のように、意味の似た単語、② purse と purser、pursuit のように形の似た単語という 2 つのパターンがあるので注意しておきましょう。

☞Check

1 ～ 3 の英文中のカッコ内から正しい語を選び○で囲みましょう。

1. I (borrowed / lent / rented) some money from the bank.
2. You'll find some money in my (purse / purser / pursuit).
3. Mr. & Mrs. Johnson decorated their house on a (little / tight / short) budget.

Part 5 Incomplete Sentences

英文を完成させるのに最も適切な語句を（A）～（D）から選びましょう。

1. Walter is an expert in finance and advises people where to ------- their money.
   - (A) interest
   - (B) invest
   - (C) inform
   - (D) inquire

2. Emma withdrew some money out of her bank ------- .
   - (A) discount
   - (B) mount
   - (C) amount
   - (D) account

3. We can expect a substantial pay raise as well as a ------- bonus this year.
   - (A) large
   - (B) heavy
   - (C) high
   - (D) tight

4. Aaron is a smart guy and organizes his financial affairs very ------- .
   - (A) absolutely
   - (B) additionally
   - (C) efficiently
   - (D) eventually

5. The new advertising campaign proved very ------- and we made lots of money.
   - (A) audible
   - (B) disposable
   - (C) profitable
   - (D) terrible

イベントの発表、告知などを扱った英文では、「〜をお知らせいたします」や「〜で開催されます」のような定型表現が数多く出てきます。こうした定型表現が語句挿入の問題に使われることもあるので、ぜひ慣れておきましょう。

☞ Check

1〜4の英文中で下線を引いた語句とその日本語訳とを線で結びましょう。

1. We <u>are pleased to announce</u> the launch of our new brand. •　　•開催される
2. Visitors <u>are encouraged to use</u> public transportation. •　　•〜にご参加ください
3. The show will <u>take place</u> in July. •　　•〜を発表いたします
4. <u>Please join us for</u> a complimentary homebuyer seminar. •　　•〜をご利用ください

Part 6　Text Completion

次の英文を読み、空所に入れるのに最も適切な語句や文を（A）〜（D）から選びましょう。

Questions 6-9 refer to the following announcement.

Free Homebuyer Seminars

Thinking about buying your first home? Please join us for a complimentary homebuyer seminar hosted by FIRST Mortgage. This seminar will give you the opportunity ------- questions, learn with the experts and get the most current information on everything you need to know about buying your home.
6.

At ------- seminar, you'll learn about various mortgage loan products. ------- . Learn about the various types of real estate loan products available to you.
7.　　　　　　　　　　　　　　　　　　　　　　　　　8.

Please join us! ------- the information you need, we'll treat you to warm hospitality, refreshments, and the chance to win prizes!
9.

6. (A) ask
　　(B) to ask
　　(C) asking
　　(D) asked

7. (A) you
　　(B) its
　　(C) their
　　(D) our

8. (A) Unfortunately, no home loans are available to you.
　　(B) Get this mobile app now!
　　(C) All home loans are not alike!
　　(D) Watch this page for the next events.

9. (A) In addition to
　　(B) Instead of
　　(C) In regard to
　　(D) Due to

eメールと並び、手紙もよく出題される文書形式の1つです。eメールと似ていますが、レターヘッドからeメールよりも多くの情報を得ることができます。次の書式例で特徴に慣れておきましょう。

手紙の書式例

UNC Financial Corporation	
1010 GRAND AVE KANSAS CITY, MO 64106	■レターヘッド 差出人の会社名、住所、電話番号などが記されます。
Ms. Hannah Hoffman 511 Delaware St Suite 200, Kansas City, MO 64105	■宛先の氏名・住所 宛先の氏名、住所が記されます。
July 13	■日付
Dear Ms. Hoffman,	■本文 最初に、宛名が記されます。 次に、用件が述べられますが、多くの場合、「導入⇒本論⇒結論」という流れになります。
Sincerely,	結びは、(Yours) Sincerely のほか、(Best) Regards などもよく使われます。
Anthony Dawson Anthony Dawson Manager UNC Financial Corporation	■差出人の署名等 差出人の署名、氏名、所属（役職、部署、会社名など）が記されます。
Enclosure	■同封物の有無

Part 7 Reading Comprehension

次の英文を読み、設問に対する答えとして最も適切なものを（A）〜（D）から選びましょう。

Questions 10-13 refer to the following letter.

UNC Financial Corporation
1010 GRAND AVE
KANSAS CITY, MO 64106

August 12, 2023

Mr. John Kemper
Manager
Human Resources Department
Kansas City Life Insurance Company
8001 NW 106th St,
Kansas City, MO 64153

Dear Mr. Kemper,

I have known Alice Young for the past five years while she has worked as an administrative assistant in the accounting department. Ms. Young has been responsible for office support, including word processing, scheduling appointments and creating brochures, newsletters, and other office literature. She fulfilled her responsibilities with little supervision.

I have been consistently impressed by both Ms. Young's attitude towards her work and her performance on the job. She is willing to put in long hours if necessary to get the job done. Her interpersonal and communication skills have allowed her to develop productive working relationships with our staff.

Ms. Young has contributed a great deal to our company and we will be sorry to lose her. I can recommend her for employment without reservation. Please let me know if you need further information.

Anthony Dawson

Anthony Dawson
Manager
Accounting Department

---

10. What is the purpose of the letter?

(A) To advertise a position
(B) To apply for a job
(C) To recommend an employee for a new job
(D) To offer a job to a candidate

11. What has Ms. Young done for the past five years?

(A) She has been an administrative assistant.
(B) She has supervised Anthony Dawson.
(C) She has worked at Kansas City Life Insurance Company.
(D) She has been a chief administrative officer.

12. The word "reservation" in paragraph 3, line 2, is closest in meaning to

(A) appointment
(B) booking
(C) belief
(D) doubt

13. What is indicated about Ms. Young?

(A) She developed hostile working relationships with her colleagues.
(B) She doesn't mind working long hours if necessary.
(C) She is never willing to put in long hours on her job.
(D) She lacks interpersonal and communication skills.

Communicative Training

Part 7 で取り上げた手紙を使ってパートナーと英語で互いに質問をしてみましょう。答える際は、"Yes." や "No." だけで終わらないよう適宜、情報を追加しましょう。

Student A
Student B（パートナー）に下記の質問をしてみましょう。

Student B
Student A（パートナー）の質問に対して Part 7 の英文を見ながら答えましょう。

1. Did Mr. Kemper write the letter?
2. What company does Mr. Kemper work for?
3. How long has Mr. Dawson known Ms. Young?
4. Which company does she work for, UNC Financial Corporation or Kansas City Life Insurance Company?
5. What department does she belong to?
6. Does Mr. Dawson hesitate to recommend her for employment?
7. (You choose!)

UNIT 07 Transportation

 Vocabulary

1. 1 ～ 10 の語句の意味として適切なものを a ～ j の中から選びましょう。　　🎵 1-80

1. suspend	＿＿＿＿	a. 調査
2. commute	＿＿＿＿	b. 委員会
3. eligible	＿＿＿＿	c. 方針
4. survey	＿＿＿＿	d. （ある方向へ）進む、向かう
5. commission	＿＿＿＿	e. 通勤する、通学する
6. affect	＿＿＿＿	f. 手配
7. departure	＿＿＿＿	g. 一時停止する、一時中断する
8. policy	＿＿＿＿	h. ～に影響を与える
9. arrangement	＿＿＿＿	i. 資格のある
10. proceed	＿＿＿＿	j. 出発

2. 語群の中から適切な語句を選び、飛行機での旅に関する関連語の表を完成させましょう。

搭乗券
（　　　　　）

預け入れ荷物
（　　　　　） baggage

機内持ち込み手荷物
（　　　） baggage

超過手荷物
（　　　） baggage

出発／到着
（　　　　）／（　　　　　）

直行便／乗継便
（　　／　　　　） flight

国内便／国際便
（　　／international）flight

目的地
（　　　　）

✓international　departure　connecting　domestic　carry-on
destination　direct　check-in　boarding pass　arrival　excess

Listening Section

Part 1 解法のコツ 〈現在完了形〉

写真描写問題では、「～している」という現在進行形が中心ですが、「～してしまった」のような現在完了形が使われることもあります。〈have / has+ 過去分詞〉の部分を聞き逃さないようにしましょう。

☞**Check**

下の写真の描写として最も適切な英文を 1 ～ 4 の中から選びましょう。

1. The man has put down his shopping bags.
2. The man is putting something into a bag.
3. The man has dropped one of his bags.
4. The man is holding some bags in his hands.

Part 1 **Photographs**   🎧 1-81, 82

(A) ～ (D) の英文を聞き、写真を最も適切に描写しているものを選びましょう。

1.

(A)   (B)   (C)   (D)

Part 2 解法のコツ 　〈質問でない疑問文〉

"Why don't we ...?"（～しませんか？）のように、疑問文の形を取っていても質問しているわけではなく、実際には相手に提案したり、依頼したりする表現があります。決まり文句になっているものが多いので慣れておきましょう。

問いかけ 　　　 Why don't we take a taxi?

正解の応答例 　 That's a good idea.

Part 2 / Question-Response 　　　　　　　　　CD 1-83～86

最初に聞こえてくる英文に対する応答として最も適切なものを（A）～（C）から選びましょう。

2. Mark your answer. 　　　(A) 　　　(B) 　　　(C)
3. Mark your answer. 　　　(A) 　　　(B) 　　　(C)
4. Mark your answer. 　　　(A) 　　　(B) 　　　(C)

Part 3 解法のコツ 　〈行動の主体〉

行動の内容を問う設問には、「男性は何をすると言っているか？」のように発話者自身の行動を問うタイプと、「男性は女性に何をするように言っているか？」のように発話者が相手に依頼する行動を問うタイプの2つがあります。質問のパターンに慣れておき、どちらの行動が問われているのかが即座にわかるようにしておきましょう。

・ What does the man say he will do?
・ What does the man offer to do?

問われているのは男性の行動！

・ What does the man ask the woman to do?
・ What does the man suggest the woman do?

問われているのは女性の行動！

Part 3 / Conversations 　　　　　　　　　CD 1-87～89

会話を聞き、5～7の設問に対する解答として最も適切なものを（A）～（D）から選びましょう。

5. What are the speakers discussing?

(A) Their driver's licenses
(B) Their schedule for tomorrow night
(C) Their means of transportation
(D) Their train passes

6. What form of transportation does the woman prefer to use when they come back home?

(A) Bus
(B) Taxi
(C) Train
(D) Car

7. What does the woman say she wants to do tonight?

(A) Catch the last train
(B) Take a taxi into the city
(C) Drive her car
(D) Drink alcohol

Part 4 解法のコツ 〈交通アナウンス〉

交通機関に関するアナウンスには、下記のような基本的な流れがあるので、情報がどのような順序で出てくるか予測することができます。慣れておきましょう。

1. 呼びかけ   Attention, all passengers for the 8:42 and all subsequent trains for London.
⇒対象は乗客

2. 目的   We regret to inform you that, owing to a fire at Macclesfield, all trains on this line have now been canceled.
⇒電車の運行停止のお知らせ

3. 追加情報、注意事項
Passengers traveling to London are requested to travel via Sheffield. The next train for Sheffield will depart at 9:10 from platform 3.
⇒代替措置のお知らせ

4. 結び   We apologize for any inconvenience this may cause.
⇒お詫び

Part 4 Talks

🎵 1-90～92

トークを聞き、8～10の設問に対する解答として最も適切なものを（A）～（D）から選びましょう。

8. According to the speaker, what caused the problem?

(A) Heavy rain
(B) A power failure at Chicago station
(C) A traffic accident on the tracks
(D) A snowstorm

9. What time does the last bus leave?

(A) At 3 P.M.
(B) At 5 P.M.
(C) At 7 P.M.
(D) At 9 P.M.

10. What are passengers traveling to Chicago advised to do?

(A) Get a refund
(B) Use an emergency bus service
(C) Wait for the regular train service to resume
(D) Reserve a seat on the bus

Communicative Training

1. Part 2 のスクリプトにある最初の問いかけを使ってパートナーと英語で互いに質問をして
   みましょう。質問に答える際は、下の回答例を参考にしましょう。なお、スクリプトは教
   員から配布されます。

Student A
Student B（パート
ナー）に Part 2 の
スクリプトにある最
初の問いかけをして
みましょう。

Student B
Student A（パート
ナー）の質問に対し
て下の回答例を参考
に答えましょう。

Q2
・ええ、そうしましょう。
・ええ、良い考えですね。
・この天気ではタクシーは
　拾えないと思います。
・（You choose!）

Q3
・もちろん、構いませんよ。
・すみません、できればし
　たくないです。
・そうできればいいのです
　が（できません）。
・（You choose!）

Q4
・ありがとう。それは助か
　ります。
・ありがとうございます。
　ご親切にどうも。
・大丈夫です。父が（車で）
　迎えに来てくれますから。
・（You choose!）

2. Part 4 のスクリプトの内容について、パートナーと英語で互いに質問をしてみましょう。
   質問に答える際は、スクリプトだけを見るようにし、下の質問は見ないようにしましょう。
   なお、スクリプトは教員から配布されます。

Student A
Student B（パート
ナー）に下記の質問
をしてみましょう。

Student B
Student A（パート
ナー）の質問に対し
て Part 4 のスクリ
プトを見ながら答え
ましょう。

1. What caused the train service to Chicago to be suspended?
2. If you have tickets to Chicago, what can you take advantage of?
3. How often are emergency buses scheduled to leave?
4. If passengers want to use the emergency bus service, what
   should they do?
5. （You choose!）

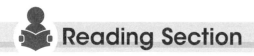

Reading Section

Part 5 解法のコツ 〈代名詞問題 1〉

選択肢に代名詞が並んでいる場合は、その代名詞が指す名詞が①単数か複数か？　②人かどうか？の２点に注意しましょう。また、下の表（一人称の代名詞）を参考にして人称代名詞・所有代名詞・再帰代名詞の働きについても確認しておきましょう。

数	人称代名詞			所有代名詞 *「〜のもの」という意味を表します。	再帰代名詞 *「〜自身」という意味を表します。
	主格 *主語として使われます。	所有格 *「〜の」という意味を表します。	目的格 *目的語として使われます。		
単数形	I	my	me	mine	myself
複数形	we	our	us	ours	ourselves

☞**Check**

1 〜 4 の英文中のカッコ内から正しい語を選び○で囲みましょう。

1. I saw a friend of (me / my / mine) off at the airport.
2. We're supposed to make (our / us / ours) own travel arrangements.
3. All of (we / our / us) are invited to the party.
4. If we sit near the front of the bus, (we / ourselves / us) will have a better view.

Part 5 Incomplete Sentences

英文を完成させるのに最も適切な語句を（A）〜（D）から選びましょう。

1. Volunteers for the event must provide ------- own transportation.

(A) they
(B) them
(C) their
(D) themselves

2. Sam never drives his car to work because ------- hates the heavy traffic in the city.

(A) he
(B) his
(C) him
(D) himself

3. I commute to work by bus, but I'm thinking of getting a car of ------- own.

(A) myself
(B) mine
(C) me
(D) my

4. The city prides ------- on great public transportation.

(A) its
(B) itself
(C) it
(D) their

5. "Thanks for your advice. But I'd rather drive than take the train."
"OK. Suit ------- ."

(A) yourself
(B) you
(C) your
(D) yours

Part 6 解法のコツ 〈群接続詞〉

語句挿入問題では、適切な接続詞を選ばせる問題がありますが、as soon as（〜したらすぐに）のような群接続詞が選択肢に並ぶことも多くあります。群接続詞とは、2語以上の単語がつながって、1つの接続詞のように使われる表現です。as long as（〜する限りは）など、頻出のものは確実にチェックしておきましょう。

☞Check

1〜4の英文中で下線を引いた語句とその日本語訳とを線で結びましょう。

1. Even if you take a taxi, you may not be able to arrive in time. •
2. We'll get there by 9:30, provided that there's a suitable train. •
3. You should have a spare tire in case you have a flat tire. •
4. I want to see Tom the moment he arrives at the station. •

• もし〜であれば
• 〜する場合に備えて
• 〜したらすぐに
• たとえ〜しても

Part 6 Text Completion

次の英文を読み、空所に入れるのに最も適切な語句や文を（A）〜（D）から選びましょう。

Questions 6-9 refer to the following notice.

Understanding Your Refund Options

If your travel plans have been affected by COVID-19, you may be eligible ------- a refund.
6.

If you have not yet canceled your trip, first cancel the reservation and request a refund. Depending on the type of ticket, you may ------- a refund back to the original form of payment.
7.

If you have already canceled your reservation, fill out the refund form. We'll contact you to let you know ------- your ticket qualifies for a refund. If your ticket qualifies, your refund will be credited back to your original form of payment. ------- .
8.   9.

Check out our refund policies for more detail.

6. (A) to
(B) on
(C) for
(D) with

7. (A) be offered
(B) offer
(C) be offering
(D) have offered

8. (A) unless
(B) whether
(C) now that
(D) as long as

9. (A) You have already received a full refund.
(B) We wish you would have contacted us sooner.
(C) Unfortunately, your ticket does not qualify for a refund.
(D) Please allow up to 7 business days for us to process your request.

81

工事や店舗開店のお知らせなど、不特定多数の人に向けた告知や案内も Part 7 ではよく出題されます。こうした告知では、記載される情報に一定の順番があるので、下の例で確認しておきましょう。問題を先読みし、どんな情報を探すべきかを頭に入れると、文書の中でどのあたりにその情報が書かれているのか見当がつくようになります。

商品回収の例

Product Recall: ChocoPets（6 oz. / 12 oz. packets）

> 最初に見出しに注目しましょう！見出しがない場合、1〜2文に案内の概要が記されます。

Briggs Chocolate is carrying out a voluntary recall of ChocoPets due to the potential presence of contaminated milk products.

> 概要に続いて、詳細や注意事項などが記されます。

For further information, please call our 24-hour hotline 1-800-555-2150, or e-mail <monsterrecall@briggs.com>.

> 最後には連絡先などが記されます。ただし、記載されない場合もあります。

次の英文を読み、設問に対する答えとして最も適切なものを（A）～（D）から選びましょう。

Questions 10-13 refer to the following notice.

Notice of Transportation Survey

In order to improve transportation services throughout the area, the Eastern Wisconsin Regional Planning Commission (EWRPC) is currently updating its long-term transportation plan, known as 2030 Urban Transportation Plan. — [1] —. As part of the ongoing project, we are conducting a survey on our citizens' transportation needs. Since transportation affects everyone in the region, feedback from citizens is very important. Please take a moment to complete the survey online at http://www. ewrpc.org/survey. — [2] —.

The EWRPC will hold a meeting on Friday, August 10, at 3 P.M. with the purpose of discussing, among other items, the results of the survey. — [3] —. The public is encouraged to attend the meeting, which will be held at the EWRPC office, 201 Delafield Street, Waukesha. The agenda and other information can be found at http://www. ewrpc.org. — [4] —.

10. What is the purpose of this notice?

(A) To introduce a new commission
(B) To announce the completion of a plan
(C) To ask citizens to complete a survey
(D) To explain the results of a survey

11. In which of the positions marked [1], [2], [3], and [4] does the following sentence best belong?
"The information we gather from the survey will help us update the plan."

(A) [1]
(B) [2]
(C) [3]
(D) [4]

12. What is indicated about the meeting?

(A) It will be held in the morning.
(B) It was held at the EWRPC office.
(C) Only members of the commission can attend the meeting.
(D) It will discuss the results of the survey.

13. What should people do if they want to obtain the agenda?

(A) Call the EWRPC office
(B) Visit the Web page of the commission
(C) Complete a survey
(D) Contact a member of the commission

Communicative Training

Part 7 で取り上げた告知を使ってパートナーと英語で互いに質問をしてみましょう。答える際は、"Yes." や "No." だけで終わらないよう適宜、情報を追加しましょう。

Student A
Student B（パートナー）に下記の質問をしてみましょう。

Student B
Student A（パートナー）の質問に対して Part 7 の英文を見ながら答えましょう。

1．What does EWRPC stand for?

2．What is the commission updating now?

3．What are they conducting a survey about?

4．What does EWRPC ask citizens to complete online?

5．When will EWRPC hold a meeting?

6．Will the results of the survey be discussed at the meeting?

7．(You choose!)

Technology

Vocabulary

1. 1 ～ 10 の語句の意味として適切なものを a ～ j の中から選びましょう。 　　🎵 2-01

1. fee	＿＿＿	a．在庫
2. package	＿＿＿	b．～を設置する、～を設定する
3. stock	＿＿＿	c．～を確認する
4. browse	＿＿＿	d．調節可能な
5. edit	＿＿＿	e．発売、公開
6. advance	＿＿＿	f．荷物、小包
7. install	＿＿＿	g．（インターネット上の情報）を閲覧する
8. adjustable	＿＿＿	h．（文書・データなど）を編集する
9. release	＿＿＿	i．進歩
10. confirm	＿＿＿	j．料金、手数料

2．語群の中から適切な日本語訳を選び、派生語の図を完成させましょう。

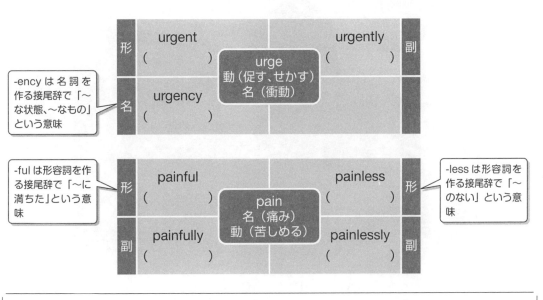

形　urgent（　　　　　）　　　urgently（　　　　　）副
-ency は名詞を作る接尾辞で「～な状態、～なもの」という意味
名　urgency（　　　　　）
urge
動（促す、せかす）
名（衝動）

-ful は形容詞を作る接尾辞で「～に満ちた」という意味
形　painful（　　　　　）　　　painless（　　　　　）形
-less は形容詞を作る接尾辞で「～のない」という意味
副　painfully（　　　　　）　　　painlessly（　　　　　）副
pain
名（痛み）
動（苦しめる）

| 緊急 | 差し迫って | 差し迫った | 無痛で | 痛みを伴う | 痛みのない | 痛切に |

Listening Section

| Part 1 | 解法のコツ | 〈受動態〉 |

物が中心の写真の場合、その状態を描写するのに受動態が多く使われます。「（物は）〜されている最中だ」という現在進行形の受動態も出題されるので、〈am / is / are+being+ 過去分詞〉の部分を聞き逃さないようにしましょう。

The books are piled up.
（本が積み重ねられています）［状態］

The plate is being washed.
（お皿は洗浄中です）［動作］

| Part 1 | Photographs |

🎧 2-02, 03

（A）〜（D）の英文を聞き、写真を最も適切に描写しているものを選びましょう。

1.

(A)   (B)   (C)   (D)

最初に聞こえてくる文は疑問文がほとんどですが、中には平叙文もあります。例えば、「このノートパソコンはどこかおかしい」と伝えることで、解決策や援助を求めるというように、何かを伝えて相手の応答を期待するタイプです。いろんなパターンがありますので、少しずつ慣れましょう。

問いかけ	Something is wrong with this laptop.
正解の応答例	Why don't you ask Bob for help?

Part 2 **Question-Response**   2-04〜07

最初に聞こえてくる英文に対する応答として最も適切なものを（A）〜（C）から選びましょう。

2. Mark your answer.　　　(A)　　　(B)　　　(C)
3. Mark your answer.　　　(A)　　　(B)　　　(C)
4. Mark your answer.　　　(A)　　　(B)　　　(C)

Part 3 解法のコツ 〈表現の言いかえ〉

正解の選択肢は、会話の中で使われていた表現をそのまま使うのではなく、別の表現で言いかえた形になっていることがよくあります。下の例では、正解の選択肢は、"Well, I'm looking for a powerful laptop." という女性の発言の下線部を a high-performance laptop と言いかえています。選択肢の中に会話で使われていた表現を見つけても、それに飛びつかないようにしましょう。

ex.)

Man:　　Welcome to First Electric. How can I help you?

Woman: Well, I'm looking for a powerful laptop. I want to edit my videos.

■ What does the woman want?

(A) Video editing software
　　　　　⇒会話で出てきた表現（edit / video）はひっかけとして使われています。

(B) A powerful vacuum cleaner
　　　　　⇒会話で出てきた表現（powerful）はひっかけとして使われています。

(C) A reasonably priced computer

(D) A high-performance laptop
　　　　　⇒正解は会話内のポイントとなる発言（下線部）を言いかえています！

Part 3 **Conversations**

 2-08～10

会話を聞き、5 ～ 7 の設問に対する解答として最も適切なものを（A）～（D）から選びましょう。

5. What is indicated about the woman's laptop?

(A) It needs to be repaired.
(B) It's old and heavy.
(C) It's heavy but very powerful.
(D) It's light but very slow.

6. What does the man ask the woman?

(A) When she bought her computer
(B) What she wants to do with her laptop
(C) Whether she has considered buying a tablet or not
(D) Whether she has edited videos or not

7. What does the man offer to do?

(A) Fix the woman's laptop
(B) Give the woman some discount coupons
(C) Show the woman some new tablets
(D) Edit the woman's photos and videos

Part 4 解法のコツ 〈留守番電話のメッセージ〉

留守番電話のメッセージには、下記のような基本的な流れがあるので、情報がどのような順序で出てくるか予測することができます。慣れておきましょう。

1. 自己紹介　This is Bill Nelson from Smart Electric.　⇒社名および氏名の連絡
2. 目的　I'm calling to confirm the delivery of your new refrigerator tomorrow afternoon.　⇒商品配達日のお知らせ
3. 追加情報、注意事項
　　Our service engineers will arrive sometime between 1 P.M. and 3 P.M. to install it.
4. 依頼事項*　If the time is inconvenient, please call our office at 555-0179.
　*必要な場合のみ　　⇒連絡先の通知

Part 4 **Talks**

 2-11～13

トークを聞き、8 ～ 10 の設問に対する解答として最も適切なものを（A）～（D）から選びましょう。

8. Why did the speaker call Scott?

(A) To ask him to buy an item at the office supply store
(B) To ask him to call the office supply store
(C) To inform him that the delivery arrived
(D) To inform him that she sent the package

9. What is the problem?

(A) An item was damaged.
(B) A wrong item was included in the package.
(C) An item wasn't delivered.
(D) The color of an item was different.

10. What is the listener asked to do?

(A) Get a refund right away
(B) Wait until the end of the month
(C) Buy the item somewhere else
(D) Return the call

Communicative Training

1. Part 2 のスクリプトにある最初の問いかけを使ってパートナーと英語で互いに質問をして
   みましょう。質問に答える際は、下の回答例を参考にしましょう。なお、スクリプトは教
   員から配布されます。

Student A
Student B（パート
ナー）に Part 2 の
スクリプトにある最
初の問いかけをして
みましょう。

Student B
Student A（パート
ナー）の質問に対し
て下の回答例を参考
に答えましょう。

Q2
- わかりました。私が見て
  あげましょう。
- あら、それはいけませ
  んね。
- 私のを使いますか？
- (You choose!)

Q3
- 了解。そうします。
- わかっていますが、私は
  マニュアルを読むのは好
  きではありません。
- もう読みました。
- (You choose!)

Q4
- それは良かったです。あ
  りがとう。
- えっ、本当に？　昨日（そ
  れを）注文したばかりで
  す。
- えっ？　最近何も注文し
  ていませんが。
- (You choose!)

2. Part 3 の対話スクリプトの内容について、パートナーと英語で互いに質問をしてみましょ
   う。質問に答える際は、対話スクリプトだけを見るようにし、下の質問は見ないようにし
   ましょう。なお、スクリプトは教員から配布されます。

Student A
Student B（パート
ナー）に下記の質問
をしてみましょう。

Student B
Student A（パート
ナー）の質問に対し
て Part 3 の対話ス
クリプトを見ながら
答えましょう。

1. What does the woman want to buy?
2. What does she say about her laptop?
3. Does she carry her laptop when she travels?
4. Has she considered buying a tablet computer yet?
5. (You choose!)

Reading Section

Part 5 　解法のコツ 　〈前置詞問題〉

前置詞は名詞・代名詞の前に置かれて、＜前置詞＋（代）名詞＞の形で形容詞や副詞の働きをするので、選択肢に前置詞が並んでいる前置詞問題では、まず空所の直後にある（代）名詞に着目しましょう。また、rely on（～に頼る）や aware of（～に気づいて）のように、動詞や形容詞とセットになって決まった意味を表す表現も出題されるので、空所の直前にも注意を払いましょう。

Check

1 ～ 4 の英文中のカッコ内から正しい語を選び○で囲みましょう。

1. I have some free time (in / at / on) the afternoon.
2. Your order is scheduled to arrive (in / at / on) the morning of October 1.
3. The plane is due (in / at / on) two hours.
4. Robert is responsible (to / for / on) recruiting and training new staff.

Part 5 　Incomplete Sentences

英文を完成させるのに最も適切な語句を（A）～（D）から選びましょう。

1. What this country needs is a long-term policy for investment ------- science and technology.

    (A) on
    (B) to
    (C) at
    (D) in

2. Many people find it difficult to keep up ------- recent technological advances.

    (A) of
    (B) to
    (C) with
    (D) for

3. Our new smartphone sold out ------- the first week after its release.

    (A) with
    (B) in
    (C) on
    (D) at

4. The company attributes its success ------- the introduction of a new wireless service.

    (A) for
    (B) with
    (C) in
    (D) to

5. ------- the introduction of new technology, the company's profits doubled last year.

    (A) Thanks to
    (B) As for
    (C) According to
    (D) Instead of

文挿入問題は語句挿入問題と比べると難易度が高いため、時間との勝負になる実際の試験では、解答の順序を最後にしたほうが得策です。文章の途中に文挿入問題があると、つい空所の順番に解きたくなりますが、語句挿入問題を優先したほうが良いでしょう。リーディングセクションでは、Part 5〜6にあまり時間をかけず、大量の英文を読まなければならない Part 7 にできるだけ多くの時間をかけるのが鉄則です。

> We spend a lot of time online every day, so we need to be careful about the personal data that we submit. But how can it be done? ---6.--- .
>
> - Create a second e-mail account for your private life. If you only use your company's e-mail address, your employer may obtain personal data from you.
> - Clear your Internet browsing history ---7.--- . The information that is stored in there can easily be accessed by certain programs.

実際の試験では、6の文挿入問題より7の語句挿入問題を先に解きましょう。

Part 6 Text Completion

次の英文を読み、空所に入れるのに最も適切な語句や文を (A) 〜 (D) から選びましょう。

Questions 6-9 refer to the following article.

How to Protect Your Privacy on the Internet

We spend a lot of time online every day, so we need to be careful about the personal data that we submit. But how can it be done? ---6.--- .

- Create a second e-mail account for your private life. If you only use your company's e-mail address, your employer may obtain personal data from you.
- Clear your Internet browsing history ---7.--- . The information that is stored in there can easily be accessed by certain programs.
- Keep important data on your private computer and ---8.--- on computers that you share with others.
- Be careful about the information you ---9.--- on Instagram and other social media.

6. (A) Cookies are small bits of information stored on your computer.
   (B) Here are some things to remember when you surf the Internet.
   (C) It collects pieces of information from your computer.
   (D) It is often installed without the knowledge of a user.

7. (A) regularly
   (B) regularity
   (C) regular
   (D) regulation

8. (A) in particular
   (B) for instance
   (C) by no means
   (D) by all means

9. (A) hide
   (B) visit
   (C) deny
   (D) disclose

Part 7 解法のコツ 〈記入用紙書式〉

スケジュール表や納品書、注文書、返品書といった表や記入用紙などもよく出題されます。これらは、比較的語数が少ないので解きやすいと言えます。また、何の文書かがわかれば内容を推測できるので、タイトルを先に確認しましょう。

APEX, INC.
ID Request Form

Please complete the top portion of this form.

> ここで ID 申請用紙であることがわかります！

Park Lane Hotel
Customer Satisfaction Survey

Please help us serve you better.

> ここで顧客満足度調査書であることがわかります！

次の英文を読み、設問に対する答えとして最も適切なものを（A）～（D）から選びましょう。

Questions 10-12 refer to the following form.

Smart Plus

2110 Pontius Ave. Los Angeles, CA 90025

www.smartplus.com

Invoice No.: y-sf-10336518

Invoice Date: October 10

Ship Date: October 12

Bill to:

Greg Palmer

2533 Robertson Blvd

Los Angeles, CA 90034

Description	Unit Price	Qty	Total
Apex Adjustable Laptop Stand	$27.99	1	$27.99
Apex R240HY 23.8-Inch Widescreen Monitor, Black	$199.99	1	$199.99
CP 64 Black Ink Cartridge	$19.95	3	$59.85
		Subtotal	$287.83
		Shipping & Handling	$15.00
		Total	$302.83

The above amount has been charged to your credit card.

Thank you for doing business with us.

---

10. What most likely is Smart Plus?

(A) A shipping company
(B) A credit-card company
(C) A photo studio
(D) An office supply store

11. What happened on October 12?

(A) The order was placed.
(B) The order was sent.
(C) The order was delivered.
(D) The order was returned.

12. What is indicated about the payment?

(A) It must be made upon receipt of goods.
(B) It must be made by the end of October.
(C) It will be made through a credit card transaction.
(D) The payment amount does not include shipping and handling fees.

Communicative Training

Part 7 で取り上げた記入用紙を使ってパートナーと英語で互いに質問をしてみましょう。答える際は、"Yes." や "No." だけで終わらないよう適宜、情報を追加しましょう。

Student A
Student B（パートナー）に下記の質問をしてみましょう。

Student B
Student A（パートナー）の質問に対して Part 7 の英文を見ながら答えましょう。

1. Who was this invoice issued to?

2. When was it issued?

3. How many ink cartridges did Mr. Palmer buy?

4. Did he buy a laptop?

5. How much does he have to pay to Smart Plus?

6. When were the items shipped?

7. (You choose!)

UNIT 09 — Health

Vocabulary

1. 1～10 の語句の意味として適切なものを a ～ j の中から選びましょう。　🔊 2-14

1. symptom	＿＿＿＿	a.	証拠
2. benefit	＿＿＿＿	b.	手術
3. prevention	＿＿＿＿	c.	要因
4. questionnaire	＿＿＿＿	d.	ウイルス
5. evidence	＿＿＿＿	e.	アンケート
6. physical	＿＿＿＿	f.	恩恵、利益
7. operation	＿＿＿＿	g.	契約書
8. virus	＿＿＿＿	h.	予防
9. factor	＿＿＿＿	i.	身体的な
10. contract	＿＿＿＿	j.	症状

2. 語群の中から適切な日本語訳を選び、派生語の図を完成させましょう。

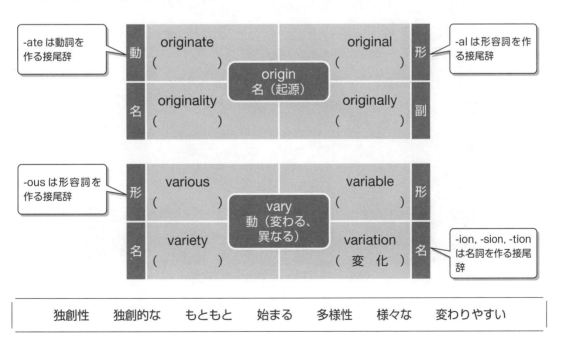

-ate は動詞を作る接尾辞

動　originate（　　　）
形　original（　　　）
origin　名（起源）
名　originality（　　　）
副　originally（　　　）

-al は形容詞を作る接尾辞

-ous は形容詞を作る接尾辞

形　various（　　　）
形　variable（　　　）
vary　動（変わる、異なる）
名　variety（　　　）
名　variation（　変化　）

-ion, -sion, -tion は名詞を作る接尾辞

独創性　　独創的な　　もともと　　始まる　　多様性　　様々な　　変わりやすい

95

Listening Section

Part 1 解法のコツ 〈様々な主語〉

複数の人物が写っている写真の場合、選択肢の主語がすべて異なる場合があります。それぞれの主語を聞き漏らさないよう、冒頭の主語に注意を払いましょう。

☞ **Check**

下の写真の描写として最も適切な英文を1～4の中から選びましょう。

1. The baby is lying on the bed.
2. The doctor is examining her patient.
3. The baby's mother is sitting up in bed.
4. They are looking in the same direction.

Part 1 Photographs

🎧 2-15, 16

（A）～（D）の英文を聞き、写真を最も適切に描写しているものを選びましょう。

1.

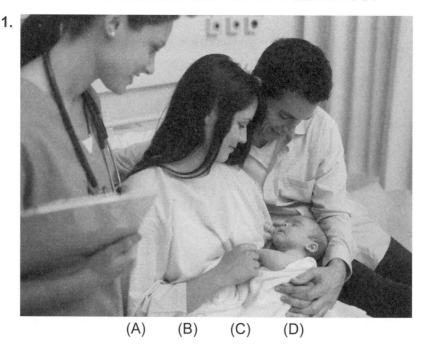

(A)   (B)   (C)   (D)

Part 2 解法のコツ 〈発音の似た単語〉

最初の問いかけに出てきた単語が含まれた選択肢は不正解である場合がほとんどですが、発音が似た単語や同じ発音で意味の異なる単語が入った選択肢も、多くの場合不正解です。

問いかけ	What seems to be the trouble?
不正解の応答例	I like to travel.
不正解の応答例	Please don't trouble yourself.
正解の応答例	I have a terrible headache.

Part 2 Question-Response

2-17〜20

最初に聞こえてくる英文に対する応答として最も適切なものを（A）〜（C）から選びましょう。

2. Mark your answer. (A) (B) (C)
3. Mark your answer. (A) (B) (C)
4. Mark your answer. (A) (B) (C)

Part 3 解法のコツ 〈場所を問う設問〉

場所に関する設問は会話が行われている場所に関するものが中心ですが、"Where will they meet?" のように話題に関するものが出題されることもあります。いずれの場合も、選択肢は場所の名前で短いものが多いので、できるだけ会話を聞く前に選択肢まで見ておくようにしましょう。会話のヒントが得られます。

· Where most likely are the speakers?
· Where is the conversation taking place?
· Where does the conversation take place?

> いずれも会話の行われている場所を尋ねる設問です。

(A) At a dry cleaner
(B) At a grocery store
(C) At a school
(D) At a hospital

> 短い選択肢が多いのでできれば事前に目を通しましょう。

会話を聞き、5〜7の設問に対する解答として最も適切なものを（A）〜（D）から選びましょう。

5. According to the man, what did the doctor say to him?

(A) His blood pressure is too high.
(B) His cholesterol level is too high.
(C) He has lost a lot of weight.
(D) He needs to put on some weight.

6. What does the man say he should do?

(A) Get more sleep
(B) Get more exercise
(C) Eat more healthily
(D) Quit smoking

7. What will the man and woman probably do next?

(A) Buy some donuts
(B) Have some coffee
(C) Work out at the gym
(D) Make some donuts

Part 4 解法のコツ 〈公共放送〉

感染症への対処など、公共性のある情報を告知する公共放送には、下記のような基本的な流れがあります。情報がどのような順序で出てくるか予測することができるので、慣れておきましょう。

1. 挨拶	This is a public health announcement.
2. 状況	As you may be aware, there has been a sharp increase in cases of the new virus.
3. 行動依頼	Wearing a mask helps prevent the spread of COVID-19.
4. 結び	Thank you for your attention.

Part 4 / **Talks** 2-24〜26

トークを聞き、8〜10の設問に対する解答として最も適切なものを（A）〜（D）から選びましょう。

8. What is this announcement about?

(A) First aid in an emergency
(B) Building tolerance for stress
(C) Heat illness prevention
(D) Flu prevention

9. What is the first piece of advice?

(A) Wear a mask
(B) Drink water
(C) Wear a hat
(D) Take breaks in the shade

10. What does the speaker suggest that the listeners do to learn more?

(A) Get a manual
(B) Call a community adviser
(C) Monitor their fellow workers
(D) Visit a Web site

Communicative Training

1. Part 2 のスクリプトにある最初の問いかけを使ってパートナーと英語で互いに質問をしてみましょう。質問に答える際は、下の回答例を参考にしましょう。なお、スクリプトは教員から配布されます。

Student A
Student B（パートナー）に Part 2 のスクリプトにある最初の問いかけをしてみましょう。

Student B
Student A（パートナー）の質問に対して下の回答例を参考に答えましょう。

Q2
・約1週間です。
・（それは）2、3日前に始まりました。
・昨日からです。
・（You choose!）

Q3
・熱があって頭痛がします。
・喉が痛いです。
・鼻水が出ます。
・（You choose!）

Q4
・はい、今朝、頭痛薬*を飲みました。
　　*headache medicine
・はい、昨夜、風邪薬*を飲みました。
　　*cold medicine
・いいえ、飲んでいません。
・（You choose!）

2. Part 3 の対話スクリプトの内容について、パートナーと英語で互いに質問をしてみましょう。質問に答える際は、対話スクリプトだけを見るようにし、下の質問は見ないようにしましょう。なお、スクリプトは教員から配布されます。

Student A
Student B（パートナー）に下記の質問をしてみましょう。

Student B
Student A（パートナー）の質問に対して Part 3 の対話スクリプトを見ながら答えましょう。

1. How did the man's health checkup go?
2. What did the doctor say about his cholesterol level?
3. Did he lose weight in the summer?
4. Which is the woman making, coffee or donuts?
5. (You choose!)

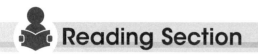

Reading Section

接続詞問題の場合、空所前後の単語に着目するのではなく、文全体を読んで内容を理解したうえで解くようにしたほうが良いでしょう。また、while と during など、意味の似通った前置詞との区別が問題になることもあり、その場合は接続詞と前置詞が選択肢に混ざった形になります。なお、接続詞と前置詞を見分けるポイントは次のとおりです。

接続詞	その後に主語と動詞を含む語句（＝節）が続きます。 ex.) Mark arrived **while** we were having dinner.
前置詞	その後に主語と動詞を含まない語句（＝句）が続きます。 ex.) Mark arrived **during** the lunch break.

☞Check

下線部に注意しながら、1 ～ 4 の英文中のカッコ内から正しい語句を選び○で囲みましょう。

1. Phillip retired early (because / because of) his poor health.
2. Computers are useful, (so / but) they may also cause various health problems.
3. Kevin was taken to the hospital (during / while) the night.
4. My high fever hasn't gone down yet, (so / because) I called in sick.

Part 5　Incomplete Sentences

英文を完成させるのに最も適切な語句を（A）～（D）から選びましょう。

1. Ted is fit and well ------- a major heart operation two years ago.
   - (A) although
   - (B) while
   - (C) because
   - (D) despite

2. ------- Dr. Harris worked at this hospital, he had received training abroad.
   - (A) After
   - (B) Prior to
   - (C) Before
   - (D) While

3. ------- you are interested in receiving free samples of our health food products, simply fill out the enclosed form.
   - (A) If
   - (B) Though
   - (C) Due to
   - (D) Before

4. ------- more public awareness of healthy eating, a lot of people are thinking more about their diet.
   - (A) Because
   - (B) Due to
   - (C) Although
   - (D) Despite

5. The air quality was so bad ------- the government issued a health warning.
   - (A) thanks to
   - (B) unless
   - (C) because
   - (D) that

語句挿入問題では、Part 5同様に前置詞問題がありますが、as for（〜に関しては）のような群前置詞が選択肢に並ぶことも多くあります。群前置詞とは、2語以上の単語がつながって、1つの前置詞のように使われる表現ですが、because of（〜のために）など、頻出のものは確実にチェックしておきましょう。

☞**Check**

1〜4の英文中で下線を引いた語句とその日本語訳とを線で結びましょう。

1. As of May 1, the firm had $5 million in long-term debt.   •   •〜を代表して
2. All utensils should be washed prior to use.   •   •〜の時点で
3. On behalf of the department I would like to thank you all. •   •〜の前に
4. I am writing with regard to your recent order.   •   •〜に関して

Part 6 / **Text Completion**

次の英文を読み、空所に入れるのに最も適切な語句や文を（A）〜（D）から選びましょう。

Questions 6-9 refer to the following e-mail.

To: All staff
From: Human Resources <hr6@joylife.com>
Date: September 13
Subject: Stress Check

Dear Colleagues,

In accordance -------- Workplace Health and Safety Regulations (2018), all
       6.
full-time JoyLife employees are required to complete an annual stress check.
In order to meet these regulations, we -------- individual online stress checks
       7.
from Wednesday, September 15 through Friday, October 1.

All information obtained in the survey is for your own guidance. In order to
access the questionnaire, double click "Application for Stress Check Survey,"
then double click the link to begin the questionnaire.

A survey manual is attached -------- your reference. -------- .
       8.   9.

Sincerely,

Cathy Goodwood
Human Resources Manager

---

6. (A) to
   (B) for
   (C) in
   (D) with

7. (A) conducted
   (B) be conducted
   (C) will conduct
   (D) conducting

8. (A) for
   (B) at
   (C) to
   (D) with

9. (A) It will remain private and confidential.
   (B) Please contact Human Resources if you require any further information.
   (C) The survey turned out to be a great success.
   (D) It may not be possible to carry out the check within this period.

Part 7　解法のコツ　〈記事書式〉

新聞や雑誌に掲載された記事は、語数が多く、語彙も難しい傾向にあります。ただし、第1段落目に全体の要旨がまとめてあるので、次のような概要に関する問題は第1段落をしっかり読めば解くことができます。諦めないようにしましょう。

　・What does the article mainly discuss?
　・What is the purpose of the article?
　・What is the article about?

> いずれも記事の概要を尋ねる設問です。

記事の例

```
              Too Much Coffee

September 15— _____
_____
_____


_____
_____
_____

_____
_____
_____
```

> 第1段落に全体の要旨がまとめてあります。最初に日付が書かれていることもあります。

次の英文を読み、設問に対する答えとして最も適切なものを（A）〜（D）から選びましょう。

Questions 10-13 refer to the following article.

Have you heard the expression "an apple a day keeps the doctor away"? While such a claim promotes a healthy lifestyle, in recent years it may well have been replaced by the belief that one route to good health is to walk 10,000 steps a day. — [1] —. However, this number of steps—equal to a distance of about 5 miles—is not based on science. It was simply a convenient number for an advertising campaign for a pedometer. And there are reasons to believe that this 10,000-step goal may be counter-productive. — [2] —.

Many people, when faced with a daily 10,000-step challenge, will find the bar too high, and will give up altogether. — [3] —. Recent research studies suggest that there are few additional benefits to be gained whether people walk 10,000 steps or only 7,000. And while walking may be an easy way to exercise, we shouldn't forget that there are many other ways to be active, and they too provide health benefits. — [4] —. The important thing is to get regular exercise. Any exercise is better than no exercise. Just don't let yourself be discouraged by big numbers and unreachable goals.

10. What does the article mainly discuss?

(A) Three steps to live a healthier life
(B) The health hazards that walking causes
(C) Various ways to boost motivation
(D) The health benefits of walking

11. The word "discouraged" in paragraph 2, line 7, is closest in meaning to

(A) disappointed
(B) disconnected
(C) distorted
(D) distracted

12. What is indicated about exercise targets?

(A) The results showed walking 7,000 steps a day can raise your risk of death.
(B) A goal of 10,000 steps a day is recommended by doctors.
(C) Higher targets have a better chance of being reached.
(D) Even if you don't reach your target, regular activity is beneficial for health.

13. In which of the positions marked [1], [2], [3], and [4] does the following sentence best belong?
"The bottom line?"

(A) [1]
(B) [2]
(C) [3]
(D) [4]

Communicative Training

Part 7 で取り上げた記事を使ってパートナーと英語で互いに質問をしてみましょう。答える際は、"Yes." や "No." だけで終わらないよう適宜、情報を追加しましょう。

Student A
Student B（パートナー）に下記の質問をしてみましょう。

Student B
Student A（パートナー）の質問に対して Part 7 の英文を見ながら答えましょう。

1. How many miles are 10,000 steps?
2. According to this article, is a 10,000-step goal based on science?
3. According to this article, does walking 10,000 steps a day provide far more benefits than walking only 7,000 steps a day?
4. What's the important thing?
5. (You choose!)

UNIT 10 Travel

 Vocabulary

1. 1 〜 10 の語句の意味として適切なものを a 〜 j の中から選びましょう。　🎧 2-27

1. itinerary	＿＿＿＿	a．革新
2. booking	＿＿＿＿	b．旅程表
3. receipt	＿＿＿＿	c．予定を再調整する
4. reimburse	＿＿＿＿	d．卒業証書
5. enthusiastic	＿＿＿＿	e．〜を延期する
6. innovation	＿＿＿＿	f．領収書
7. diploma	＿＿＿＿	g．製造する
8. reschedule	＿＿＿＿	h．（払ったお金）を払い戻す、〜に返金する
9. manufacture	＿＿＿＿	i．予約
10. postpone	＿＿＿＿	j．熱心な

2. 語群の中から適切な日本語訳を選び、派生語の表を完成させましょう。

人を表す名詞を作る主な接尾辞	もとの単語（名詞・動詞）	人を表す名詞
-ant	serve（仕える）	servant（　　　　）
-ee	examine（試験する）	examinee（　　　　）
-er		examiner（　　　　）
-ian	guard（保護する）	guardian（　　　　）
-ist	novel（　　　　）	novelist（　　　　）
-or	investigate（　　　　）	investigator（調査官）

受験者　　調査する　　保護者　　小説　　使用人　　小説家　　試験官

Listening Section

Part 1 解法のコツ 〈先入観の排除〉

写真の中で大きく写っている物にはどうしても注意が向きがちですが、必ずしもそれを描写する文が正解とは限りません。先入観を持たずにすべての文を聞いてから解答しましょう。また、写真に人が写っていても、人が主語となる文が正解とは限らない点も要注意です。

☞ Check

下の写真の描写として最も適切な英文を 1 ～ 4 の中から選びましょう。

1. The woman is sitting on her suitcase.
2. The suitcase is being opened.
3. The couch is unoccupied.
4. The woman is lying on the carpet.

Part 1 **Photographs**

2-28, 29

（A）～（D）の英文を聞き、写真を最も適切に描写しているものを選びましょう。

1.

(A)　　(B)　　(C)　　(D)

Part 2　解法のコツ　〈同一単語の繰り返し2〉

最初の問いかけに出てきた単語や発音の似た単語が入った選択肢は不正解である場合がほとんどですが、A or B という形式の選択疑問文は例外です。同じ単語が入った選択肢が正解となる場合もあるので注意しましょう。

問いかけ	Which is easier to get there, the train or the bus?
正解の応答例	The train would be much easier.

Part 2　Question-Response

 2-30～33

最初に聞こえてくる英文に対する応答として最も適切なものを（A）～（C）から選びましょう。

2. Mark your answer.　　　(A)　　　(B)　　　(C)
3. Mark your answer.　　　(A)　　　(B)　　　(C)
4. Mark your answer.　　　(A)　　　(B)　　　(C)

Part 3　解法のコツ　〈話者を問う設問〉

話し手の職業を尋ねる設問の場合、選択肢は職業名が並び、短いものが多いので、できるだけ会話を聞く前に選択肢まで見ておくようにしましょう。会話のヒントが得られます。また、"Who most likely is the man?" のようにストレートに職業名を尋ねる質問もあれば、"Where does the man most likely work?" のように勤務先を尋ねる質問もあります。

・Who most likely is the man?

(A) A travel agent
(B) A server
(C) A hotel receptionist
(D) A bookkeeper

・Where does the man most likely work?

(A) At a travel agency
(B) At a restaurant
(C) At a hotel
(D) At a conference center

> 短い選択肢が多いので、できれば事前に目を通しましょう。

Part 3　Conversations

2-34～36

会話を聞き、5～7の設問に対する解答として最も適切なものを（A）～（D）から選びましょう。

5. Where does the man most likely work?

(A) At a travel agency
(B) At a restaurant
(C) At a hotel
(D) At a conference center

6. According to the woman, what is the problem?

(A) There is no king-sized bed.
(B) There is only one bed.
(C) The air-conditioner isn't working.
(D) The room is dirty.

7. What does the man say he will do?

(A) Check the woman's booking
(B) Send someone to her room
(C) Call the woman back later
(D) Talk to the manager

Part 4 解法のコツ   〈図表問題 1〉

Part 3 同様に、Part 4 でも図表付きの問題が出題されます。3 つの設問のうち図表に関するものは 1 つで、"Look at the graphic." という指示が設問の冒頭に書かれています。トークを聞く前に、図表を見て何が書いてあるのか確認しておきましょう。

工場見学の地図だとわかります！

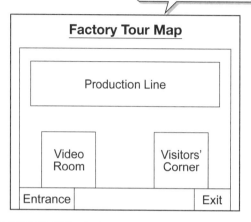

10. Look at the graphic. Where will the listeners receive a free sample?

(A) At the Video Room
(B) At the Production Line
(C) At the Visitors' Corner
(D) At the Exit

Part 4 Talks

 2-37～39

トークを聞き、8 ～ 10 の設問に対する解答として最も適切なものを（A）～（D）から選びましょう。

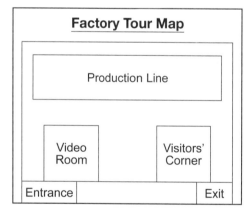

8. Where does the speaker work?

(A) At an electronics company
(B) At a confectionery company
(C) At a drug company
(D) At a beverage company

9. What will listeners do in the visitors' corner?

(A) Learn the history of the company
(B) See how the products are manufactured
(C) Answer a questionnaire
(D) Create their own candy bars

10. Look at the graphic. Where will the listeners receive a free sample?

(A) At the Video Room
(B) At the Production Line
(C) At the Visitors' Corner
(D) At the Exit

Communicative Training

1. Part 2 のスクリプトにある最初の問いかけを使ってパートナーと英語で互いに質問をしてみましょう。質問に答える際は、下の回答例を参考にしましょう。なお、スクリプトは教員から配布されます。

Student A
Student B（パートナー）に Part 2 のスクリプトにある最初の問いかけをしてみましょう。

Student B
Student A（パートナー）の質問に対して下の回答例を参考に答えましょう。

Q2
・そうですね、私は電車のほうがいいです。
・タクシーに乗りませんか？
・私はどちらでもいいです。
・（You choose!）

Q3
・もうありません。すみません。
・すみません、よくわかりません。
・すみません、誰か他の人に聞いてもらえませんか？
・（You choose!）

Q4
・私はオーシャンビューのほうがいいです。
・どちらでもいいです。私は気にしません。
・どちらのほうが安いですか？
・（You choose!）

2. Part 4 のスクリプトの内容について、パートナーと英語で互いに質問をしてみましょう。質問に答える際は、スクリプトだけを見るようにし、下の質問は見ないようにしましょう。なお、スクリプトは教員から配布されます。

Student A
Student B（パートナー）に下記の質問をしてみましょう。

Student B
Student A（パートナー）の質問に対して Part 4 のスクリプトを見ながら答えましょう。

1. Who is the guide of the chocolate factory tour?
2. What will the tour participants watch at the beginning of the tour?
3. Where will they create their own candy bars?
4. What will they get at the end of the tour?
5. (You choose!)

Reading Section

動詞の形を問う問題で選択肢に ing 形があった場合、現在分詞と動名詞の 2 つの可能性があるので注意しましょう。動名詞は、「〜すること」のように動詞を名詞化するものですが、動詞が名詞の働きをするものには to 不定詞もあるので、この 2 つの使い分けにも慣れておく必要があります。

👉 Check

1 〜 4 の英文中のカッコ内から正しい語を選び○で囲みましょう。

1. (Reserve / Reserving) airline tickets online has become very popular.
2. Our travel agent advised us (to take / taking) a direct flight instead of a connecting flight.
3. More and more people are (travel / traveling) with their pets.
4. I can't imagine (travel / traveling) around the world.

Part 5 Incomplete Sentences

英文を完成させるのに最も適切な語句を（A）〜（D）から選びましょう。

1. According to the survey, about half of the business travelers questioned said they expected ------- less for business.

(A) travel
(B) to travel
(C) traveling
(D) traveled

2. I'm considering ------- a new suitcase for my business trip abroad.

(A) buy
(B) buying
(C) to buy
(D) bought

3. The company will reimburse you for travel expenses, so don't forget ------- your receipts during your trip next week.

(A) keep
(B) keeping
(C) to keep
(D) kept

4. First-class hotels are all fully ------- during the height of the tourist season.

(A) book
(B) booked
(C) to book
(D) booking

5. My trip to the U.K. has been postponed, but I'm looking forward ------- you again.

(A) to seeing
(B) see
(C) to see
(D) seeing

求人案内などを扱った英文では、「仕事内容には〜が含まれます」や「応募者には〜が必要です」のような定型表現が数多く登場します。こうした定型表現が語句挿入問題や文挿入問題に使われることもあるので、ぜひ慣れておきましょう。

☞ Check

1 〜 4 の英文中で下線を引いた語句とその日本語訳とを線で結びましょう。

1. Fluency in Japanese <u>is preferred but not required</u>. •   • 職務には〜が含まれます
2. <u>Applicants must have</u> at least three years of experience as a tour guide.   • 応募者には〜が必要です
3. <u>Duties include</u> supervising tour guides.   • 採用者には〜が必要です
4. <u>The successful candidate will have</u> a university degree in tourism.   • 望ましいですが必須ではありません

Part 6 / **Text Completion**

次の英文を読み、空所に入れるのに最も適切な語句や文を（A）〜（D）から選びましょう。

Questions 6-9 refer to the following advertisement.

Savannah Tours has an immediate opening for enthusiastic tour guides! We provide our customers with memorable tours and our guides play a large role in that process. The tour guide is responsible for making sure that our tours are ------- , informative, and memorable. No experience is necessary and an 8-week training period will be provided.
<small>6.</small>

The successful candidate will be able to effectively communicate with the public and fellow employees. ------- . A university degree is preferred, but candidates with high school diplomas are also eligible.
<small>7.</small>

Interested individuals ------- to send an e-mail with their résumé to Steve Thompson, the personnel director, at <sthompson@savannahtours.com>. Applications must be submitted by December 10 at ------- .
<small>8.</small> <small>9.</small>

6. (A) entertaining
  (B) entertain
  (C) entertained
  (D) entertainer

7. (A) Applications received after this deadline will not be read.
  (B) We often made recommendations on sites to see, restaurants to visit, as well as give directions.
  (C) We are currently seeking a tour guide and details will be given at interview.
  (D) In addition, the ability to retain historical information is necessary.

8. (A) encourage
  (B) are encouraged
  (C) are encouraging
  (D) encouraged

9. (A) late
  (B) later
  (C) the latest
  (D) lately

ダブルパッセージ問題では、両方の文書を読まないと解けない形式の問題（クロスレファレンス問題）が必ず含まれます。次の例では、文書Aで会議の開始時間を読み取り、文書Bでスミス氏が30分遅れることを読み取って初めて正解の（D）にたどり着けます。慣れるまでは難しいですが、問題を数多くこなしながらコツを掴みましょう。

What time will Mr. Smith attend the meeting?
(A) 2:00
(B) 2:30
(C) 3:00
(D) 3:30

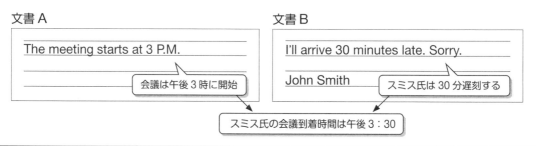

Part 7　**Reading Comprehension**

次の英文を読み、設問に対する答えとして最も適切なものを（A）〜（D）から選びましょう。

Questions 10-14 refer to the following itinerary and e-mail.

Itinerary for Edward Feldman

Thursday, October 28	Sydney	Retail Innovation Conference
Monday, November 1	Perth	Meeting with Mr. George Anton of Global, Inc.
Wednesday, November 3	Melbourne	Visit several shopping malls, including Royal Arcade
Thursday, November 4	Melbourne	Meeting with Ms. Katy Gilligan of Coles, Inc.
Friday, November 5	Home	

To:	Jane Larson
From:	Edward Feldman
Date:	October 21
Subject:	My trip to Australia
Attachment:	Itinerary

Morning Jane,

The itinerary (attached) for my upcoming trip to Australia has been finalized. I'll be back in my office on November 8, not 5. Could you please take care of the following for me while I'm away?

1. I'll be needing the latest sales figures when I meet with Ms. Gilligan, but I don't think they will be available by the end of this month. Please let me know as soon as they're ready. Tom is in charge of coming up with the figures, so ask him for details.
2. I don't think I'll be able to meet David Olson in my office on November 5. Please reschedule the appointment with him. I'll be available all day on November 8 and 9.

Just let me know if you have questions or need further information.
Thanks.

Edward

10. What company does Ms. Gilligan work for?

(A) Global, Inc.
(B) Royal Arcade
(C) Retail Innovation
(D) Coles, Inc.

11. By when does Mr. Feldman need to get the latest sales figures?

(A) November 1
(B) November 3
(C) November 5
(D) November 8

12. In the e-mail, the word "figures" in paragraph 2, line 1, is closest in meaning to

(A) expense
(B) forecast
(C) numbers
(D) force

13. According to the e-mail, what is stated about Tom?

(A) He knows details about the sales figures.
(B) He won't be available until the end of the month.
(C) He will be attending Retail Innovation Conference.
(D) He is supposed to meet Mr. Feldman on November 5.

14. In the e-mail, what is Ms. Larson asked to do?

(A) Provide the sales figures to Mr. Olson
(B) Meet Mr. Feldman at the airport
(C) Reschedule an appointment
(D) Accompany Mr. Feldman to Australia

Communicative Training

Part 7 で取り上げた旅程表を使ってパートナーと英語で互いに質問をしてみましょう。答える際は、"Yes." や "No." だけで終わらないよう適宜、情報を追加しましょう。なお、スクリプトは教員から配布されます。

Student A
Student B（パートナー）に下記の質問をしてみましょう。

Student B
Student A（パートナー）の質問に対して Part 7 の英文を見ながら答えましょう。

1. When will Mr. Feldman arrive in Sydney?
2. What day of the week is it?
3. What is he going to attend in Sydney?
4. What city is he going to visit after Sydney?
5. What city is his final destination in Australia?
6. Does Mr. Anton work for Coles, Inc.?
7.（You choose!）

Business

 Vocabulary

1. 1〜10の語句の意味として適切なものを a 〜 j の中から選びましょう。　

2-40

1. admit	＿＿＿	a．緊急な
2. renovation	＿＿＿	b．拡大する
3. supplier	＿＿＿	c．修正、（書物の）改訂
4. overview	＿＿＿	d．概観、概要
5. divide	＿＿＿	e．修繕、リフォーム
6. urgent	＿＿＿	f．供給業者、納入元
7. reorganization	＿＿＿	g．一時解雇
8. layoff	＿＿＿	h．〜を認める
9. revision	＿＿＿	i．〜を分割する
10. expand	＿＿＿	j．再編成、改組

2. 語群の中から適切な語句を選び、会議に関する関連語の表を完成させましょう。

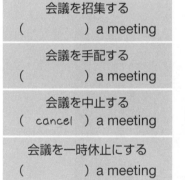

会議を招集する （　　　　）a meeting	会議の日程を変更する （　　　　）a meeting
会議を手配する （　　　　）a meeting	会議に参加する （　　　　）a meeting
会議を中止する （ cancel ）a meeting	会議を終わらせる （　　　　）a meeting
会議を一時休止にする （　　　　）a meeting	会議を延期する （　　／　　）a meeting

✓cancel　　attend　　adjourn　　wrap up　　put off　　reschedule

call　　postpone　　arrange

Listening Section

Part 1 解法のコツ 〈人物（3人以上）の描写2〉

3人以上の人物が写っている写真の場合、全員の共通点を描写するものが多いですが、特定の人物の動作や服装、持ち物などの描写が正解となる場合もあります。

☞ Check

下の写真の描写として最も適切な英文を1～4の中から選びましょう。

1. A man is writing something on the whiteboard.
2. They're all seated at a table.
3. A man is talking to a group of people.
4. They're all looking at the whiteboard.

Part 1 / **Photographs**

2-41, 42

（A）～（D）の英文を聞き、写真を最も適切に描写しているものを選びましょう。

1.

(A)　　(B)　　(C)　　(D)

"Do you know where he lives?" のように、疑問文を平叙文の語順にして目的語や補語として使うタイプ（間接疑問文）では、途中に出てくる疑問詞が聞き取りのポイントになります。聞き逃さないようにしましょう。

問いかけ	Can you tell me when the manager will be back?
不正解の応答例	Yes, the manager is Mr. Lloyd.
正解の応答例	He'll be back by five.

Part 2 Question-Response 2-43〜46

最初に聞こえてくる英文に対する応答として最も適切なものを（A）〜（C）から選びましょう。

2. Mark your answer.   (A)   (B)   (C)
3. Mark your answer.   (A)   (B)   (C)
4. Mark your answer.   (A)   (B)   (C)

会話の話題を問う設問では、"What is the conversation mainly about?" や "What are the speakers discussing?" のように、何について話しているかをストレートに問うものが中心となります。しかし、この他にも "What is the problem?" や "What is wrong with the project?" のように、話題となっている問題点を具体的に問う形式もありますので慣れておきましょう。

- What is the conversation mainly about?
- What are the speakers discussing?   「何についての会話か？」
- What is wrong with the project?
- According to the man, what is the problem?   「（話題となっている）問題点は何か？」

Part 3 Conversations   2-47〜49

会話を聞き、5〜7の設問に対する解答として最も適切なものを（A）〜（D）から選びましょう。

5. What are the speakers discussing?

  (A) Their new boss
  (B) The starting date of a new project
  (C) The budget for the next year
  (D) Business with their customer

6. According to the man, what is the problem?

  (A) The completion date has already passed.
  (B) He has trouble contacting Jerry.
  (C) They have overspent on this project.
  (D) They haven't found any supplier yet.

7. What does the woman ask the man to do?

  (A) Bring Jerry here
  (B) Change the completion date
  (C) Discuss the problems with Jerry
  (D) Think of a new budget plan

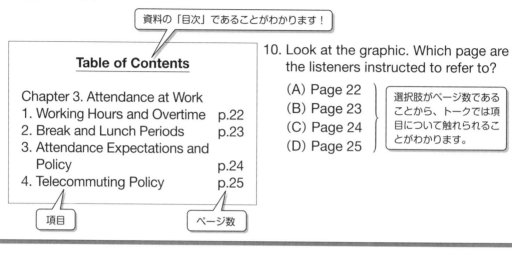

Part 4 解法のコツ 〈図表問題2〉

図表付きの問題では、トークを聞く前に図表を見て何が書いてあるのか確認しておきましょう。また、図表に関する設問の選択肢に目を通しておくと、トークの中で図表に関してどういった情報が出てくるか予想できます。

> 資料の「目次」であることがわかります！

Table of Contents

Chapter 3. Attendance at Work
1. Working Hours and Overtime　p.22
2. Break and Lunch Periods　p.23
3. Attendance Expectations and Policy　p.24
4. Telecommuting Policy　p.25

> 項目

> ページ数

10. Look at the graphic. Which page are the listeners instructed to refer to?

(A) Page 22
(B) Page 23
(C) Page 24
(D) Page 25

> 選択肢がページ数であることから、トークでは項目について触れられることがわかります。

Part 4 Talks

 2-50～52

トークを聞き、8～10の設問に対する解答として最も適切なものを（A）～（D）から選びましょう。

Table of Contents

Chapter 3. Attendance at Work
1. Working Hours and Overtime　p.22
2. Break and Lunch Periods　p.23
3. Attendance Expectations and Policy　p.24
4. Telecommuting Policy　p.25

8. What is the talk about?

(A) An update about the hiring plan
(B) The new inspection manual
(C) Revisions to the employee manual
(D) Telephone use policy

9. Why does the speaker say, "but if you don't, just raise your hand"?

(A) To encourage the listeners to ask questions
(B) To see if everyone has the material
(C) To ask the listeners to support his plan
(D) To check attendance

10. Look at the graphic. Which page are the listeners instructed to refer to?

(A) Page 22
(B) Page 23
(C) Page 24
(D) Page 25

1. Part 2 のスクリプトにある最初の問いかけを使ってパートナーと英語で互いに質問をして
   みましょう。質問に答える際は、下の回答例を参考にしましょう。なお、スクリプトは教
   員から配布されます。

Student A
Student B（パート
ナー）に Part 2 の
スクリプトにある最
初の問いかけをして
みましょう。

Student B
Student A（パート
ナー）の質問に対し
て下の回答例を参考
に答えましょう。

Q2
・人事部のホフマンさん
　（女性）です。
・わかりません。
・ベンに聞いてもらえませ
　んか？　彼が知っている
　はずです。
・（You choose!）

Q3
・2 階の会議室です。
・それは 5 階の会議室で開
　かれます。
・よくわかりません。すみ
　ません。
・（You choose!）

Q4
・あら、（それらは）私の
　です。どこで見つけたの
　ですか？
・すみません。わかりませ
　ん。
・ルークのでしょう。彼は
　鍵を探していましたから。
・（You choose!）

2. Part 4 のスクリプトの内容について、パートナーと英語で互いに質問をしてみましょう。
   質問に答える際は、スクリプトだけを見るようにし、下の質問は見ないようにしましょう。
   なお、スクリプトは教員から配布されます。

Student A
Student B（パート
ナー）に下記の質問
をしてみましょう。

Student B
Student A（パート
ナー）の質問に対し
て Part 4 のスクリ
プトを見ながら答え
ましょう。

1. What is the first item on the agenda?
2. What are the listeners supposed to bring with them?
3. Only one small change was made in the latest manual, wasn't it?
4. Was the biggest change made to telecommuting?
5. (You choose!)

Reading Section

通常、語彙問題の選択肢は 1 語ですが、次の例のように 2 語以上の場合もあります。

At present, we are (running into / looking for / putting on / taking off) a larger office space.

この場合、〈動詞 + 前置詞・副詞〉で特別な意味を持つ句動詞の知識が問われています。上記の問題の場合、「〜を探す」という意味を持つ look for の活用形である looking for が正解になります。語彙学習の際には、こうした句動詞にも目を向けましょう。

☞Check

1 〜 4 の英文中で下線を引いた語句とその日本語訳とを線で結びましょう。

1. Brian will take over this project.　　　　　•　　　• 断った
2. We need to carry out more research.　　　•　　　• 引き継ぐ
3. Sarah turned down a job at an investment bank.　•　• 延期する
4. We decided to put off the meeting.　　　　•　　　• 行う

Part 5 Incomplete Sentences

英文を完成させるのに最も適切な語句を（A）〜（D）から選びましょう。

1. Joseph admitted that something urgent had come up, but he ------- the details.

    (A) turned on
    (B) took over
    (C) got on
    (D) held back

2. They employed Eleanor because of her excellent skill in ------- the press.

    (A) dealing with
    (B) turning in
    (C) putting on
    (D) carrying on

3. Mr. White asked me to ------- the shop while he was out.

    (A) take after
    (B) count on
    (C) look after
    (D) turn down

4. Employees at Triton Bank fear that the bank's reorganization will ------- layoffs.

    (A) look for
    (B) get over
    (C) put off
    (D) result in

5. We cannot ------- the task any longer. The deadline is the end of this month.

    (A) make out
    (B) put off
    (C) carry out
    (D) call on

手紙や e メールでは、「よろしくお願いいたします」や「お返事をいただければ幸いです」のような定型表現が数多く登場します。こうした定型表現に慣れておくと、素早く長文を読むことができるようになるので、ぜひ慣れておきましょう。

☞ Check

1 〜 4 の英文中で下線を引いた語句とその日本語訳とを線で結びましょう。

1. Please find attached our new company
   brochure.
2. I look forward to hearing from you.
3. Thank you for your inquiry.
4. Thank you in advance.

- ・お問い合わせありがとうございます
- ・よろしくお願いいたします
- ・〜を添付いたします
- ・お返事をいただければ幸いです

Part 6　Text Completion

次の英文を読み、空所に入れるのに最も適切な語句や文を（A）〜（D）から選びましょう。

Questions 6-9 refer to the following e-mail.

To: Cathy Ashfield <cashfield@northernshipping.com>
From: John Freeman <jfreeman@global-tech.com>
Date: July 18
Subject: Re: Company Name Change

Dear Ms. Ashfield,

I'm writing to inform you that we have recently changed the name of ------- 6. business from Southern Engineering Ltd. to Global Technologies Corp.

As the new name shows, we intend to further expand our global business from now on. However, there has been no change in management and we ------- 7. to provide the same quality products and services. Our new company brochure is attached to this e-mail for your ------- 8. .

------- 9. .

Yours sincerely,

John Freeman
President
Global Technologies Corporation

6. (A) we
   (B) ours
   (C) our
   (D) us

7. (A) will continue
   (B) continuing
   (C) continued
   (D) had continued

8. (A) trouble
   (B) reference
   (C) patience
   (D) advice

9. (A) I would like to ask you a favor.
   (B) We are deeply sorry for your loss.
   (C) Thank you for your inquiry regarding our products.
   (D) Thank you for being one of our valued customers.

オンラインチャットは、基本的に、シングルパッセージ問題の前半に2人のやりとりが1題、後半に3人以上のやりとりが1題出題されます。2人のやりとりは短くて取り組みやすいものが多いですが、3人以上のやりとりは複雑なので、人物関係を把握するように努めましょう。下の例では、リンダとマークのやりとりに途中からジェイが加わっています。呼びかけの言葉に注意して、話の流れを掴みましょう。

オンラインチャットの例

Linda Midler [11:08] Hi, Mark. _____
Mark Jordan [11:10] _____
Linda Midler [11:11] _____
Mark Jordan [11:13] _____
Linda Midler [11:14] _____
Mark Jordan [11:16] _____
Linda Midler [11:18] I just can't edit the file for some reason.
Mark Jordan [11:22] Let me check with Jay. Jay, I just sent Linda a link to the presentation slides, but she can't edit them.
Jay Foster [11:25] OK. I'll look into it right away.
_____
_____

マークは「ジェイに確かめさせてください」とリンダに伝え、それからジェイに話しかけています。Jayという呼びかけに注意しましょう。

Part 7　Reading Comprehension

次の英文を読み、設問に対する答えとして最も適切なものを（A）〜（D）から選びましょう。

Questions 10-13 refer to the following chat discussion.

John Wells (10:12 A.M.)
Hi, Robert and Anne. We need to find a place for the staff meeting next week.

Robert Baxter (10:14 A.M.)
Why? Can't we use the conference room?

John Wells (10:15 A.M.)
No. Didn't you see the e-mail from Luke? The room is being renovated all next week.

Robert Baxter (10:16 A.M.)
Yeah, I remember. Then, how about the seminar room on the seventh floor? It's too big for our meeting, but it can be divided into two rooms.

John Wells (10:19 A.M.)
It's already reserved.

Anne Powell (10:20 A.M.)
Could we have the meeting in the cafeteria? It's big enough and we can move the chairs and tables around.

John Wells (10:23 A.M.)
Well, that might work. But can we reserve the space for a meeting?

Anne Powell (10:24 A.M.)
I can ask Luke. He should know about that.

John Wells (10:25 A.M.)
Could you ask him?

Anne Powell (10:27 A.M.)
Sure thing. I'll call him up now and will get back to you soon.

---

10. What is the chat discussion mainly about?

(A) An agenda for the meeting
(B) Members for the meeting
(C) Renovation of a room
(D) A reservation

11. According to the chat, what is indicated about the conference room?

(A) It can be divided into two rooms.
(B) It is on the seventh floor.
(C) It will not be available next week.
(D) It has been renovated.

12. The word "renovated" in paragraph 3, line 2, is closest in meaning to

(A) repaired
(B) reserved
(C) destroyed
(D) required

13. At 10:27 A.M., what does Ms. Powell most likely mean when she writes, "Sure thing"?

(A) She is sure that Luke knows about that.
(B) She is willing to contact Luke.
(C) She will move the chairs and tables around soon.
(D) She will go to the cafeteria right away.

Communicative Training

Part 7 で取り上げたチャットを使ってパートナーと英語で互いに質問をしてみましょう。答える際は、"Yes." や "No." だけで終わらないよう適宜、情報を追加しましょう。

Student A
Student B（パートナー）に下記の質問をしてみましょう。

Student B
Student A（パートナー）の質問に対してPart 7の英文を見ながら答えましょう。

1. What does Mr. Wells say they need to find?
2. Why can't they use the conference room?
3. On what floor is the seminar room?
4. Can the seminar room be divided into two rooms?
5. Can they reserve the seminar room?
6. Where does Ms. Powell suggest that they should have the meeting?
7. (You choose!)

UNIT 12 Entertainment

 Vocabulary

1. 1～10の語句の意味として適切なものを a～j の中から選びましょう。　🎵 2-53

1. acclaim	＿＿＿＿	a．評論家、批評家
2. particularly	＿＿＿＿	b．(チケットなどが)有効な、期限切れでない
3. celebration	＿＿＿＿	c．落ち着く、定住する
4. explore	＿＿＿＿	d．祝賀、祝うこと
5. valid	＿＿＿＿	e．遠足、外出
6. critic	＿＿＿＿	f．(努力など)に報いる
7. reward	＿＿＿＿	g．～を称賛する
8. settle	＿＿＿＿	h．特に、とりわけ
9. vehicle	＿＿＿＿	i．(通常陸上の)乗物、輸送機関
10. outing	＿＿＿＿	j．～を探索する

2. 語群の中から適切な日本語訳を選び、派生語の表を完成させましょう。

名詞を作る主な接尾辞	もとの単語（動詞・形容詞）	名詞
-ence	refer（参照する）	reference（　　　　）
-ency	emergent（緊急な）	emergency（　　　　）
-ness	weak（弱い）	weakness（　　　　）
-ion, -sion, -tion	object（反対する）	objection（　　　　）
-ment	argue（　　　　）	argument（　　　　）
-ity, -ty	diverse（　　　　）	diversity（　　　　）
-ance	attend（出席する）	attendance（　　　　）

緊急事態　　多様性　　反対　　参考・参照　　弱点　　出席
多様な　　議論　　言い争う

125

Listening Section

Part 1 解法のコツ 〈種類を表す名詞〉

写真に写っている物を描写する際に、具体的な名前を挙げずに種類を表す名詞で表現することがあります。例えば、piano の代わりに musical instrument（楽器）を使う場合などです。こうした種類を表す名詞にも慣れておきましょう。

☞ **Check**

1〜6 の語句とその種類を表す語句を線で結びましょう。

1. couch	•	• musical instrument
2. coffee	•	• electrical appliance
3. trumpet	•	• beverage
4. trousers	•	• clothing
5. vacuum cleaner	•	• vehicle
6. truck	•	• furniture

Part 1 **Photographs**

2-54, 55

（A）〜（D）の英文を聞き、写真を最も適切に描写しているものを選びましょう。

1.

(A)　　(B)　　(C)　　(D)

Part 2	解法のコツ	〈あいまいな応答〉

問いかけに対して、「どちらでも構わない」、「別の人に聞いてほしい」、「もう少し考えさせてほしい」のように、あいまいな応答が正解となることもあります。

問いかけ	Why don't we go to the music festival this weekend?
正解の応答例	Let me think about it for a while.

Part 2	Question-Response

 2-56〜59

最初に聞こえてくる英文に対する応答として最も適切なものを（A）〜（C）から選びましょう。

2. Mark your answer.　(A)　(B)　(C)
3. Mark your answer.　(A)　(B)　(C)
4. Mark your answer.　(A)　(B)　(C)

Part 3	解法のコツ	図表問題 2

図表問題は、会話から得られる情報と図表から得られる情報を組み合わせないと解けない仕組みになっています。図表問題の場合、図表にざっと目を通し、どんな情報が載っているのかを会話が流れてくる前に確認しておきましょう。

 図表の情報：座席表

6. Look at the graphic. Where will the speakers sit?
(A) In Section A
(B) In Section B
(C) In Section C
(D) In Section D

Part 3	Conversations

 2-60〜62

会話を聞き、5〜7の設問に対する解答として最も適切なものを（A）〜（D）から選びましょう。

Seating Chart

Stage

A	B	C

D

Entrance　　　　　　　　　　Exit

6. Look at the graphic. Where will the speakers sit?

(A) In Section A
(B) In Section B
(C) In Section C
(D) In Section D

5. What are the speakers planning to attend?

(A) A concert
(B) A play
(C) A ceremony
(D) A film festival

7. What does the man ask the woman to do?

(A) Pay for his ticket
(B) Meet him at the entrance
(C) Introduce him to Emily
(D) Give his best to Emily

ラジオ放送には、下記のような基本的な流れがあるので、情報がどのような順序で出てくるか予測することができます。慣れておきましょう。

1. 挨拶、番組紹介　　You're listening to the morning show on Radio KABC.
　　　　　　　　　　　⇒ラジオ局、番組名などの紹介
2. 目的　　　　　　　I'm Sally Davis with the weather report.
　　　　　　　　　　　⇒天気予報のお知らせ
3. 詳細　　　　　　　It's very cold and windy today. There is a chance of some rain in the afternoon too, so don't leave home without your umbrella!
　　　　　　　　　　　⇒寒くて、風が強く、午後には雨の可能性
4. 次の情報の紹介　　Now, here's Tom Jones with the traffic updates for today.
　　　　　　　　　　　⇒次は交通情報

Part 4 **Talks**

 2-63〜65

トークを聞き、8 〜 10 の設問に対する解答として最も適切なものを（A）〜（D）から選びましょう。

8. What will be held this Saturday?

(A) A film festival
(B) A music festival
(C) A sports game
(D) A play

9. What is indicated about the event?

(A) It will start at noon and go on all afternoon.
(B) Susan Gilbert will host the event.
(C) It is held once a year.
(D) Admission is free and no tickets are necessary.

10. What will you most likely hear after this talk?

(A) A weather report
(B) A traffic report
(C) Sports news
(D) Entertainment news

Communicative Training

1. Part 2 のスクリプトにある最初の問いかけを使ってパートナーと英語で互いに質問をしてみましょう。質問に答える際は、下の回答例を参考にしましょう。なお、スクリプトは教員から配布されます。

Student A
Student B（パートナー）に Part 2 のスクリプトにある最初の問いかけをしてみましょう。

Student B
Student A（パートナー）の質問に対して下の回答例を参考に答えましょう。

Q2
・ここで買えますよ。
・あいにく売り切れました。
・オンラインで買えますよ。
・（You choose!）

Q3
・とても良かったです。
・まあまあでした。
・思っていたより良かったです。
・（You choose!）

Q4
・私はテレビを見たいです。
・そうですね、今は仕事をしなければいけません。
・そうですね、映画に行きませんか？
・（You choose!）

2. Part 4 のスクリプトの内容について、パートナーと英語で互いに質問をしてみましょう。質問に答える際は、スクリプトだけを見るようにし、下の質問は見ないようにしましょう。なお、スクリプトは教員から配布されます。

Student A
Student B（パートナー）に下記の質問をしてみましょう。

Student B
Student A（パートナー）の質問に対して Part 4 のスクリプトを見ながら答えましょう。

1. What's the name of the event?
2. Do you need tickets?
3. How much are they?
4. Where can you get them?
5. （You choose!）

Reading Section

George devoted (him / himself / his / he) to his latest album.

この問題は、選択肢を見ると代名詞問題と言えますが、devote oneself to（〜に専念する）という慣用句の知識があればすぐに解けます。語彙学習の際は単語だけでなく、こうした慣用句にも注意を払いましょう。

☞ Check

1〜4の英文中で下線を引いた語句とその日本語訳を線で結びましょう。

1. I can't <u>make sense of</u> that film.　　　　　　　　•　　　　•〜と対立して

2. The actor and the director are <u>at odds with</u> each other. •　　•〜を犠牲にして

3. Are you going to <u>take part in</u> that movie audition?　　•　　•〜を理解する

4. Janet enjoyed her popularity <u>at the cost of</u> her privacy. •　•〜に参加する

Part 5 ｜ Incomplete Sentences

英文を完成させるのに最も適切な語句を（A）〜（D）から選びましょう。

1. I take pride ------- my work—particularly my work as a film director.

(A) off
(B) in
(C) to
(D) on

2. The group has decided not to release any new songs for the time ------- .

(A) be
(B) been
(C) to be
(D) being

3. One day, out of the ------- , the famous actress announced her retirement.

(A) blue
(B) red
(C) world
(D) question

4. It is by no ------- certain that the film festival will take place.

(A) charge
(B) chance
(C) means
(D) name

5. Let's take ------- of the vacation to visit every museum in the city.

(A) care
(B) effect
(C) aim
(D) advantage

Unit 3、5 で 2 つの文をつなぐ主な副詞（句）を確認したので、実際の問題形式で確認してみましょう。結果（したがって）、逆接（しかし）、情報追加（さらに）、例示（例えば）、順序（最初に）のように、パターンが決まっているので、問題演習を繰り返して慣れましょう。

☞ **Check**

空所に当てはまる語句を語群から選んで、1 〜 2 の英文を完成させましょう。

1. His latest film was highly acclaimed among the critics. (   ), it turned out to be a box office failure.

2. All employees receive paid holiday and sick leave. (   ), we offer various benefits for new parents.

語群

Therefore	However	In addition	For example	First

Part 6 **Text Completion**

次の英文を読み、空所に入れるのに最も適切な語句や文を（A）〜（D）から選びましょう。

Questions 6-9 refer to the following e-mail.

To: All employees
From: Jack Houston <jhouston@dataquick.com>
Date: October 20
Subject: Company outing

Dear Employees,

We are pleased to announce that our company outing ------- place on Saturday, October 30 to thank you for the hard work you've put in over the past year. This also serves as the company's celebration of ------- recent expansion.
6.
7.

We will be having a barbecue party at Greenstone National Park. Games, raffles, and other fun activities will fill the day. ------- , you can enjoy a picnic, a tug-of-war, canoeing, and so on.
8.

------- . If you are bringing your family members or friends, please fill in the number of people who will attend.
9.

Hope to hear from you.

Regards,

Jack Houston
Manager
General Affairs Department
Data Quick, Inc.

6. (A) took
   (B) has taken
   (C) will take
   (D) will be taken

7. (A) your
   (B) my
   (C) its
   (D) their

8. (A) However
   (B) Then
   (C) On the contrary
   (D) For example

9. (A) This is to reward you for your hard work.
   (B) Please use the attached Excel file to sign up.
   (C) Unfortunately, we canceled our company outing due to heavy rain.
   (D) We are looking forward to meeting you in your new office.

Part 7 解法のコツ 〈キーワードに関する設問〉

Part 7 では限られた時間で大量の英文を読まなければならないので、文書を読む前に設問を読んでおき、解答に必要な情報だけを探すつもりで文書を読んでいく必要があります。その際、次に挙げるような設問の場合、A にあたる語句がキーワードになるので、文書を読む際には A を探し、そこに書かれている内容を素早く読み取りましょう。

・What is indicated about A?
・What is stated about A?
・What is true about A?
・What is suggested about A?

> いずれも A に関して書かれていることを探しましょう！

Part 7 Reading Comprehension

次の英文を読み、設問に対する答えとして最も適切なものを（A）～（D）から選びましょう。

Questions 10-13 refer to the following Web page.

HUDDSVILLE BOOKS

| ONLINE EVENTS | BESTSELLERS | FICTION | NON-FICTION | CHILDREN'S | CONTACT US |

I'll Drink to That!
—An online interview with author David Clayton

Join us for a really exciting event with explorer, adventurer and storyteller David Clayton, as he talks to TV personality Donna Cherie about his new book *I'll Drink to That!* This superb follow-up to his bestselling *Climb Every Mountain* is packed with stories that will either take your breath away or make you laugh!

Attacked by bandits in the jungles of Brunei? Arrested on three continents while cycling around the world? David has done it all and lived to tell the tale. — [1] —.

David Clayton has been exploring and risking his life for nearly half a century. He has now settled into a quiet life of writing—at least until he begins his next crazy adventure. Be sure to meet him now while you still have the chance!

Book your ticket today! — [2] —.
Date & Time: Tuesday, January 19, 18:00
Price: $20 Event & signed copy of *I'll Drink to That!*
$10 Event only
Note: — [3] —. This is an online event. It was originally scheduled for December 11 but was rescheduled to the current date following David's recent accident. — [4] —.

10. What is mentioned about David?

(A) He has been exploring for more than 50 years.
(B) His next book *Climb Every Mountain* will be published soon.
(C) He wrote the book *I'll Drink to That* with Donna Cherie.
(D) He had an accident recently.

11. The word "superb" in paragraph 1, line 3, is closest in meaning to

(A) excellent
(B) new
(C) timely
(D) notorious

12. What is indicated about the online event?

(A) At least $20 is necessary to join it.
(B) It will be held on the weekend.
(C) TV personality Donna Cherie will interview David Clayton.
(D) The first event held on December 11 turned out to be a great success.

13. In which of the positions marked [1], [2], [3], and [4] does the following sentence best belong?
"Tickets purchased for the original date will still be valid for this event."

(A) [1]
(B) [2]
(C) [3]
(D) [4]

Communicative Training

Part 7 で取り上げたウェブページを使ってパートナーと英語で互いに質問をしてみましょう。
答える際は、"Yes." や "No." だけで終わらないよう適宜、情報を追加しましょう。

Student A
Student B（パートナー）に下記の質問をしてみましょう。

Student B
Student A（パートナー）の質問に対して Part 7 の英文を見ながら答えましょう。

1. Who is Donna Cherie?
2. Who is she going to interview?
3. Will the interview be held face-to-face or online?
4. Which is Mr. Clayton's latest book, *I'll drink to that!* or *Climb Every Mountain*?
5. Will the interview be held on the weekend?
6. What day was it originally scheduled for?
7. (You choose!)

UNIT 13 Education

Vocabulary

1. 1 〜 10 の語句の意味として適切なものを a 〜 j の中から選びましょう。　2-66

1. credit	＿＿＿＿	a．学期
2. strategy	＿＿＿＿	b．共同設立者
3. registration	＿＿＿＿	c．集中的な
4. compliance	＿＿＿＿	d．〜を受け入れる、〜を引き受ける
5. honor	＿＿＿＿	e．（科目の）履修単位
6. accept	＿＿＿＿	f．（規則などに対する）順守
7. practical	＿＿＿＿	g．〜に名誉を授ける
8. intensive	＿＿＿＿	h．履修登録
9. co-founder	＿＿＿＿	i．戦略
10. semester	＿＿＿＿	j．実用的な

2．語群の中から適切な日本語訳を選び、派生語の図を完成させましょう。

動詞を作る 接尾辞・接頭辞*	もとの単語（名詞・形容詞）	動詞
-ate	active（　　　　）	activate（　　　　）
-en	strength（強さ）	strengthen（　　　　）
-fy, -ify	just（正しい）	justify（　　　　）
-ize	memory（記憶）	memorize（　　　　）
en-	courage（　　　　）	encourage（　　　　）

勇気づける　　暗記する　　活性化する　　正当化する　　勇気 強くする　　活動的な

Note　接頭辞とは、unable の un- など、語の先頭に付けられて、その語の意味あるいは機能を変える要素を指します。

Listening Section

写真の中で目立つものはキーワードになりやすいですが、多くの場合、複数の選択肢で使われます。最初に聞こえてきたものに飛びつかず、すべての選択肢を確認したうえで解答しましょう。

Check

下の写真の描写として最も適切な英文を 1 ～ 4 の中から選びましょう。

1. The girl is buying a mask.
2. The girl is raising her hand.
3. The girl is putting on a mask.
4. The girl is wearing a mask.

> キーワードは mask ですが、3 つの文に使われており、正答の決め手になるのは下線部です。

Part 1 Photographs   2-67, 68

（A）～（D）の英文を聞き、写真を最も適切に描写しているものを選びましょう。

1.

(A)   (B)   (C)   (D)

Wh 疑問文や Yes / No 疑問文が中心になるので、出だしに着目することが重要ですが、主語が何かも確認しておきましょう。"Yes, I did." が正解となるべき質問に対して、"Yes, he did." のように、主語が間違っている選択肢が用意されていることがあります。

問いかけ	When is this assignment due?
不正解の応答例	They're due next week.
正解の応答例	Next Wednesday.

Part 2 Question-Response

2-69〜72

最初に聞こえてくる英文に対する応答として最も適切なものを（A）〜（C）から選びましょう。

2. Mark your answer.　　(A)　　(B)　　(C)
3. Mark your answer.　　(A)　　(B)　　(C)
4. Mark your answer.　　(A)　　(B)　　(C)

Part 3 解法のコツ 〈3 人での会話〉

会話は基本的に 2 人ですが、全部で 13 ある会話のうち 2 つ程度は 3 人の会話となっています。その場合、"Questions XX through XX refer to the following conversation with three speakers." という指示文が会話の前に流れ、3 人の会話であることがわかるようになっています。2 人の会話と 3 人の会話で解き方に大きな違いはありませんが、1 人しかいない性別に関する設問が多いので、その人の発言に注意しましょう。また、設問に具体的な人名が出てくることも特徴の 1 つです。

ex.）男性 2 名、女性 1 名の会話における設問例
・Who is the woman?　　　　⇒ 1 名しか登場しない性別に関する設問が目立つ！
・What is indicated about Jeff? ⇒同じ性別が複数いるため、人名が記載されることが多い！

Part 3 Conversations

2-73〜75

会話を聞き、5 〜 7 の設問に対する解答として最も適切なものを（A）〜（D）から選びましょう。

5. What are the speakers talking about?

(A) Their reports
(B) Their registration
(C) Their grades
(D) Their examination schedule

6. What is the deadline?

(A) Yesterday
(B) Today
(C) Tomorrow
(D) The day after tomorrow

7. What is indicated about Ethan?

(A) He will have a busy schedule.
(B) His grades were better than he expected.
(C) He hasn't registered yet.
(D) He will turn in his reports tomorrow.

Part 4 解法のコツ 〈人物紹介スピーチ〉

表彰式や講演会などでこれから登場する人を紹介するスピーチには、下記のような基本的な流れがあるので、情報がどのような順序で出てくるか予測することができます。慣れておきましょう。

1. 呼びかけ	Good evening, everyone. Welcome to the special lecture meeting by Dayton College.
2. 目的	Tonight, we are honored to have with us Dr. John Kerrigan. ⇒ゲストの紹介
3. 追加情報	He's the co-founder of the World Science Festival and the author of many best-selling scientific books. ⇒肩書、経歴、テーマなど、ゲストに関する追加情報の紹介
4. 結び	Please give a very warm welcome to Professor John Kerrigan. ⇒ゲストへのバトンタッチ

Part 4 Talks

 2-76〜78

トークを聞き、8 〜 10 の設問に対する解答として最も適切なものを（A）〜（D）から選びましょう。

8. Where does the speaker work?

(A) At a university
(B) At a radio station
(C) At a bookstore
(D) At a TV station

9. What will Dr. Foster most likely talk about?

(A) How to become a psychologist
(B) How to write a bestseller
(C) His recent trip
(D) Good ways to sleep well

10. What does the speaker encourage listeners to do?

(A) Send questions for the guest
(B) Answer a questionnaire
(C) Come to the studio
(D) Study at Brighton University

Communicative Training

1. Part 2 のスクリプトにある最初の問いかけを使ってパートナーと英語で互いに質問をしてみましょう。質問に答える際は、下の回答例を参考にしましょう。なお、スクリプトは教員から配布されます。

Student A
Student B（パートナー）に Part 2 のスクリプトにある最初の問いかけをしてみましょう。

Student B
Student A（パートナー）の質問に対して下の回答例を参考に答えましょう。

Q2
・あら、それは素晴らしいですね。どこに行きたいのですか？
・どれくらい滞在する予定ですか？
・実は、私もそれを考えているのです。
・（You choose!）

Q3
・はい、昨日申し込みました。
・いいえ、まだです。
・いいえ、まだそれについて考えているところです。
・（You choose!）

Q4
・会議室*で開催される予定です。
　　　*conference room
・よくわかりません。すみません。
・ご案内します。私について来てください。
・（You choose!）

2. Part 3 の対話スクリプトの内容について、パートナーと英語で互いに質問をしてみましょう。質問に答える際は、対話スクリプトだけを見るようにし、下の質問は見ないようにしましょう。なお、スクリプトは教員から配布されます。

Student A
Student B（パートナー）に下記の質問をしてみましょう。

Student B
Student A（パートナー）の質問に対して Part 3 の対話スクリプトを見ながら答えましょう。

1. Does registration end today?
2. How many classes has Jake signed up for?
3. How many credits will he get if he passes all the classes?
4. Has Ethan signed up yet?
5. (You choose!)

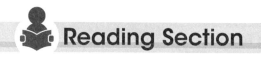

Reading Section

Part 5 解法のコツ　〈代名詞問題 2〉

代名詞問題には、人称代名詞の他に関係代名詞も含まれます。関係代名詞の問題の場合は、まず空所の前を見て、先行詞にあたる名詞（句）が人であるか、それとも人以外であるかを確認します。次に、空所の後の部分がどのような構造になっているかを見極めましょう。

また、下の図を参考にして主な関係代名詞について確認しておきましょう。

先行詞	主格	所有格	目的格
人	who	whose	who / whom
人以外	which	whose	which
人・人以外	that	−	that

> 目的格の関係代名詞は省略されることもあります。

☞Check

下線部に注意して、1 〜 4 の英文中のカッコ内から正しい語を選び○で囲みましょう。

1. Anyone (what / whose / who) wants to sign up for this course must do so by Friday.
2. Did you hear (what / that / which) Professor Morrison just said?
3. I helped a classmate (who / whose / which) laptop had broken down.
4. Joe's parents, (who / that / whose) are both teachers, work at the same high school.

Part 5 Incomplete Sentences

英文を完成させるのに最も適切な語句を（A）〜（D）から選びましょう。

1. Jack drove past his old school, ------- is celebrating its 50th anniversary this year.

   (A) what
   (B) who
   (C) which
   (D) that

2. This intensive course is designed for those ------- have little or no computer experience.

   (A) which
   (B) whose
   (C) who
   (D) what

3. The Career Center will provide the support and resources ------- you need to make your career search successful.

   (A) who
   (B) what
   (C) whose
   (D) that

4. This school is only for students ------- first language is not English.

   (A) who
   (B) whose
   (C) whom
   (D) their

5. Jennifer's son got accepted at the college ------- went to about 30 years ago.

   (A) she
   (B) that
   (C) who
   (D) him

2 つの文をつなぐ主な副詞（句）については、これまで取り上げたもの以外に、「その一方で」や「それどころか」のように「対比」を表すものもあります。実際の問題形式で確認してみましょう。

☞Check

空所に当てはまる語句を語群から選んで、1 ～ 2 の英文を完成させましょう。

1. The teacher wasn't happy. (　　　　　), he was mad.
2. Getting good grades is important. (　　　　　), it isn't everything.

語群

| On the contrary | On the one hand | However | For instance |

Part 6 Text Completion

次の英文を読み、空所に入れるのに最も適切な語句や文を（A）～（D）から選びましょう。

Questions 6-9 refer to the following e-mail.

Dear Professor Brown:

Thank you very much for honoring me with an invitation to lecture at your university. ----6.---- normal conditions I would have been more than happy to accept.

Unfortunately, I will be on an overseas business trip during the dates you ----7.---- for your program, so I cannot accept this time. However, I do hope that you will consider me for one of your future programs.

----8.---- . Please feel free to call on me if there is some other way in which I can be of ----9.---- .

Yours sincerely,

Sarah Parker

---

6. (A) With
   (B) While
   (C) Unless
   (D) Under

7. (A) will propose
   (B) proposed
   (C) proposing
   (D) to propose

8. (A) I wish you every success with your program.
   (B) I deeply apologize for the error I have made.
   (C) We're pleased to hear that your program was a great success.
   (D) I wish you would refrain from contacting me anymore.

9. (A) assist
   (B) assistant
   (C) assistance
   (D) assists

Part 7 は限られた時間で大量の英文を読む必要があるので時間との戦いになります。その中でも特に時間がかかるのが、「〜でないものはどれですか？」というタイプの設問です。選択肢 (A) 〜 (D) のそれぞれについて文書の中に記載があるかどうかを確認していかなければならないので、どうしても解答に時間がかかります。実際の試験の場合にはこうした設問は後回しにするなどして時間を有効に活用しましょう。

設問例

・What is NOT true about A?

・What is NOT mentioned as a feature of A?

・What does NOT apply to A?

> 時間がない時は「〜でないもの」タイプの設問は後回しにするのも１つの手段です！

Part 7　Reading Comprehension

次の英文を読み、設問に対する答えとして最も適切なものを（A）〜（D）から選びましょう。

Questions 10-14 refer to the following brochure and e-mail.

East Melbourne University
Group Program

Human Resource Management Program

This 5-day course is designed for Human Resources personnel looking to further develop their skills in Human Resources and Management.

Program objectives

This is a practical program that develops knowledge, skills and professional practice for Human Resources (HR) professionals. The participants will learn:

• Workforce planning strategies,
• HR systems and compliance issues,
• Performance management systems,
• Organizational culture and change.

Timetable

Time \ Day	MONDAY	TUESDAY	WEDNESDAY	THURSDAY	FRIDAY
AM	Orientation and tour of campus	Lecture 2: Workforce planning strategies	Lecture 3: HR systems and compliance issues	Lecture 4: Performance management systems	Lecture 5: Organizational culture and change
PM	Lecture 1: Introduction to Human Resource Management	Culture: Walking tour of Melbourne city	Networking with current students	Industry visit: Related government bodies	Debrief session and farewell

Contact us

If you have any questions or would like to discuss the proposal, please contact us at <groupprograms@emu.edu.au>.

To:	groupprograms@emu.edu.au
From:	h.saunders@randolph-e.com
Date:	January 28
Subject:	Human Resource Management Program

Dear Sir or Madam,

I'm interested in your Human Resource Management Program. Currently I manage the Human Resources department at an engineering company in Melbourne, and I'm thinking of having our 10 employees in the department take this program as part of our training program. The timetable of the program is excellent, but since we are based in Melbourne, a walking tour of the city does not really seem to suit our needs. Is it possible to replace the tour with something directly related to Human Resource Management?

Hope to hear from you.

Kind regards,

Hank Saunders
Director
Human Resources
Randolph Engineering Pty. Ltd.

10. Who is the brochure directed to?

(A) Workers in personnel departments
(B) People interested in natural resource management
(C) High school graduates
(D) Retired employees

11. On the brochure, what is NOT indicated about the program?

(A) Participants will learn performance management systems.
(B) Participants will have the opportunity to visit related government bodies.
(C) The duration of the program is five days.
(D) All the lectures will be provided in the morning.

12. What is the purpose of the e-mail?

(A) To recommend a lecturer
(B) To make an inquiry
(C) To make an appointment
(D) To sign up for a course

13. In the e-mail, what does Mr. Saunders refer to?

(A) The program on Tuesday
(B) The program on Wednesday
(C) The program on Thursday
(D) The program on Friday

14. What is true about Mr. Saunders?

(A) He has taken the program before.
(B) He is in charge of one of the five lectures.
(C) He is the president of an engineering company.
(D) He works at a company in Melbourne.

Communicative Training

Part 7 で取り上げたパンフレットを使ってパートナーと英語で互いに質問をしてみましょう。
答える際は、"Yes." や "No." だけで終わらないよう適宜、情報を追加しましょう。

Student A
Student B（パートナー）に下記の質問をしてみましょう。

Student B
Student A（パートナー）の質問に対して Part 7 の英文を見ながら答えましょう。

1. Is this program designed for sales professionals?
2. How long does it last?
3. How many lectures are included in the program?
4. Are all the lectures conducted in the morning?
5. What day of the week is networking with current students held?
6. Is the orientation held in the afternoon?
7. (You choose!)

UNIT 14 Housing

 Vocabulary

1. 1 ～ 10 の語句の意味として適切なものを a ～ j の中から選びましょう。　　🎧 2-79

1. resident	＿＿＿	a.	移行、過渡期
2. affordable	＿＿＿	b.	～を確実にする
3. landlord	＿＿＿	c.	～を更新する
4. improvement	＿＿＿	d.	手ごろな価格の
5. ensure	＿＿＿	e.	広々とした
6. transition	＿＿＿	f.	居住者
7. luxury	＿＿＿	g.	改良、改修（工事）
8. renew	＿＿＿	h.	豪華な
9. lease	＿＿＿	i.	賃貸借契約
10. spacious	＿＿＿	j.	家主、大家

2. 語群の中から適切な日本語訳を選び、派生語の図を完成させましょう。

形容詞を作る主な接尾辞	もとの単語（名詞・動詞）	形容詞
-able	value（価値）	valuable（　　　　）
-al	nation（国家・国民）	national（　　　　）
-ed	refine（洗練する）	refined（　　　　）
-ent	insist（主張する）	insistent（　　　　）
-ful	harm（害）	harmful（　　　　）
-ic	hero（英雄）	heroic（　　　　）
-ical	type（種類・型）	typical（　　　　）
-ing	rule（統治する）	ruling（　　　　）
-ive	create（創造する）	creative（　　　　）
-less	flaw（欠点）	flawless（　　　　）

有害な	執拗な	支配的な	国家の	洗練された
創造的な	欠点のない	典型的な	価値がある	英雄的な

Listening Section

Part 1 解法のコツ 〈物の状態〉

〈物〉が中心の写真の場合には、その「位置」と「状態」を確認しましょう。位置関係は、前置詞がポイントになりますが、状態について「積み重ねられている」、「立て掛けられている」などの頻出表現をチェックしておきましょう。

Chairs are piled up / stacked.
（椅子が積み重ねられています）

A ladder is leaning
against the wall.
（はしごが壁に立て掛けられています）

Books are lined up in a row.
（本が一列に並べられています）

Part 1 Photographs

2-80, 81

（A）〜（D）の英文を聞き、写真を最も適切に描写しているものを選びましょう。

1.

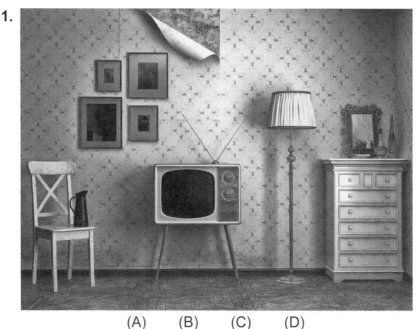

(A)　　(B)　　(C)　　(D)

Part 2 解法のコツ 〈質問で返す応答〉

問いかけに対して、「誰から聞いたのですか？」のように、質問で返す応答が正解となる場合があります。自然なやりとりになるように、最初の問いかけから対話の場面を想像することが大切です。

問いかけ	Did you move to a new apartment?
正解の応答例	How did you know that?

Part 2 Question-Response　 2-82〜85

最初に聞こえてくる英文に対する応答として最も適切なものを（A）〜（C）から選びましょう。

2. Mark your answer.　　(A)　　(B)　　(C)
3. Mark your answer.　　(A)　　(B)　　(C)
4. Mark your answer.　　(A)　　(B)　　(C)

Part 3 解法のコツ 〈意図を問う設問〉

設問の中には、会話で使われた表現を引用し、「〜と言った時、男性は何を意味していますか？」のように、話者の意図を尋ねるものがあります。文字どおりの意味ではなく、会話の文脈の中でその表現がどのように使われているかをよく考えましょう。また、こうした設問には次のようないくつかのパターンがあります。

・What does the woman mean when she says, "Let me sleep on it"?
　　　　　　　　　　　　　　　　　⇒「何を意味しているのか？」
・What does the woman imply when she says, "Let me sleep on it"?
　　　　　　　　　　　　　　　　　⇒「何をほのめかしているのか？」
・Why does the woman say, "Let me sleep on it"?　⇒「なぜ〜と言うのか？」

Part 3 Conversations　 2-86〜88

会話を聞き、5〜7の設問に対する解答として最も適切なものを（A）〜（D）から選びましょう。

Floor Plan

	Apartment 3	Apartment 4
Apartment 2		
	Apartment 1	

▲Stairs

5. Look at the graphic. Which apartment are the speakers talking about?

(A) Apartment 1
(B) Apartment 2
(C) Apartment 3
(D) Apartment 4

6. What is indicated about the apartment?

(A) It was renovated last year.
(B) It's very popular.
(C) It's next to the stairs.
(D) It's on the third floor.

7. What does the woman mean when she says, "Let me sleep on it"?

(A) She'd like to make an offer.
(B) She needs some rest now.
(C) She'll think it over.
(D) She won't make an offer.

Part 4 解法のコツ 〈広告〉

商品やサービスの広告に関するトークの場合、相手の注意を引くために最初の呼びかけで概要がわかるようになっています。下記が基本的な流れなので、特に出だしに注意して聞くようにしましょう。

1. 呼びかけ	Looking for your dream house?	
	⇒対象は家の購入を検討している人	
2. 自己紹介	Dream Realty can help you find a house that best suits you.	
	⇒会社の紹介	
3. 詳細	We are proud to announce our prestigious new development, Caldwell Estate.	
	⇒分譲団地の紹介	
4. 結び	Come join us for our Open House on Sunday, July 12.	
	⇒聞き手への提案	

Part 4 Talks

 2-89〜91

トークを聞き、8 〜 10 の設問に対する解答として最も適切なものを（A）〜（D）から選びましょう。

8. Who is this talk directed to?

(A) People who want to rent or purchase a house
(B) People who wish to work at Dream Property
(C) People who plan to make some improvements on their house
(D) People who are interested in selling their house

9. What is indicated about Dream Property?
(A) It specializes in affordable housing.
(B) It has several branch offices.
(C) Its head office is in Woodfield Mall.
(D) It will celebrate its first anniversary on March 3.

10. What can customers do on Saturday?

(A) Enjoy free refreshments
(B) Get a special discount
(C) Celebrate the opening of the Woodfield Mall
(D) Get a gift card

Communicative Training

1. Part 2のスクリプトにある最初の問いかけを使ってパートナーと英語で互いに質問をして
   みましょう。質問に答える際は、下の回答例を参考にしましょう。なお、スクリプトは教
   員から配布されます。

Student A
Student B（パート
ナー）に Part 2 の
スクリプトにある最
初の問いかけをして
みましょう。

Student B
Student A（パート
ナー）の質問に対し
て下の回答例を参考
に答えましょう。

Q2
・わかりました。予算はい
　かほどでしょうか？
・わかりました。特にご希
　望のエリアはございます
　か？
・そうですね、これはいか
　がでしょうか？
・（You choose!）

Q3
・月 600 ドルです。
・昨年と同じです。
・よくわかりません。確認
　させてください。
・（You choose!）

Q4
・いいえ、特にありません。
・そうですね、駅の近くに
　住みたいです。
・そうですね、どのエリア
　が人気ありますか？
・（You choose!）

2. Part 3の対話スクリプトの内容について、パートナーと英語で互いに質問をしてみましょ
   う。質問に答える際は、対話スクリプトだけを見るようにし、下の質問は見ないようにし
   ましょう。なお、スクリプトは教員から配布されます。

Student A
Student B（パート
ナー）に下記の質問
をしてみましょう。

Student B
Student A（パート
ナー）の質問に対し
て Part 3 の対話ス
クリプトを見ながら
答えましょう。

1. Does the woman think the apartment is too small?
2. What does she say about the view from the apartment?
3. On what floor is the apartment?
4. Is there an elevator in the apartment building?
5. (You choose!)

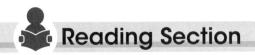# Reading Section

「仕事から帰宅したらあなたに電話します」における「仕事から帰宅したら」の部分は未来のことを指していますが、"I'll call you when I get home from work." のように現在形を使います。このように、時を表す when や条件を表す if などで始まる副詞節では、未来のことであっても現在時制を使うので注意しましょう。ただし、名詞節の場合には、未来のことを表す場合には will を使うので気をつけてください。

> 2つ以上の単語のまとまりが1つの品詞と同じ働きをするもののうち、主語と動詞を含むものを節と呼び、主語と動詞を含まないものは句と呼びます。

副詞節	副詞の役割を果たす節で、修飾語になります。 ex.) I'll call you **when I get home from work**.
名詞節	名詞の役割を果たす節で、主語や目的語、補語になります。 ex.) I don't know **when he'll get home from work**.

☞Check

1〜3の英文中のカッコ内から正しい語句を選び○で囲みましょう。

1. I'll e-mail you when I (decide / will decide) to rent the apartment.
2. Do you know when the house (is / will be) offered for sale?
3. We have to stay in temporary accommodation until our house (will be / is) rebuilt.

Part 5 **Incomplete Sentences**

英文を完成させるのに最も適切な語句を（A）〜（D）から選びましょう。

1. Let's wait here until the real estate agent ------- back.

- (A) come
- (B) will come
- (C) came
- (D) comes

2. We have received so many inquiries about the office for rent that we don't know when we ------- able to finish answering them.

- (A) have been
- (B) were
- (C) will be
- (D) are

3. Our house ------- recently, so now it's a two-family house.

- (A) renovated
- (B) was renovated
- (C) will renovate
- (D) was renovating

4. We're not going to renew our apartment lease unless the landlord ------- to lower the rent.

(A) agrees
(B) agree
(C) will be agreeing
(D) agreed

5. The rent on the apartment was lower than we expected, so we ------- to sign the lease on the spot.

(A) decide
(B) decided
(C) were deciding
(D) had decided

Part 6　解法のコツ　　〈定型表現 4〉

保守点検の告知などを扱った英文では、「ご不便をおかけし、申し訳ございません」や「ご協力のほど、よろしくお願い申し上げます」のような定型表現が数多く登場します。こうした定型表現が語句挿入の問題に使われることもあるので、ぜひ慣れておきましょう。

☞ Check

1 〜 4 の英文中で下線を引いた語句とその日本語訳を線で結びましょう。

1. Please <u>be informed that</u> on Tuesday, November 7 there will be a scheduled power outage.　　•　　• ご迷惑

2. Thank you for your <u>patience</u> and understanding.　　•　　• 〜をお知らせします

3. Our Web site will be <u>temporarily unavailable</u>.　　•　　• ご辛抱

4. We apologize for any <u>inconvenience</u> this may cause.　•　　• 一時的に利用不可

151

次の英文を読み、空所に入れるのに最も適切な語句や文を（A）〜（D）から選びましょう。

Questions 6-9 refer to the following notice.

Water Supply Suspended

All residents,

This is ------- all residents that the water supply will be suspended for five
hours (10 A.M. to 3 P.M.) on Monday, January 20 ------- the cleaning of the
water tank. All residents are advised to store water for the day. ------- . Thank
you for your understanding and ------- .

---

6. (A) inform
   (B) informing
   (C) informed
   (D) to inform

7. (A) by
   (B) on
   (C) for
   (D) until

8. (A) We apologize in advance for any inconvenience that may be caused.
   (B) In addition, we are very pleased to have received good feedback from you.
   (C) However, our Web site will not be available during this time.
   (D) First, you need to save water.

9. (A) cooperate
   (B) cooperation
   (C) cooperative
   (D) cooperatively

トリプルパッセージ問題では、クロスレファレンス問題が5問中2〜3問含まれます。1つの問題を解くのに3つの文書A〜Cのすべてから情報を組み合わせないといけないことはまれです。1つの文書を読めば解ける形式、もしくは、文書Bと文書Cのように、2つの文書に含まれる情報を組み合わせて解く形式になっており、基本的にはダブルパッセージ問題と変わりません。ただし、やはり難しいですので、少しずつ慣れていきましょう。

文書A（eメール1）

From: Harold Chasen
To: All staff
Date: May 16
Subject: New staff member

Dear colleagues,
_____
Maude will be starting work with us next month.
_____
_____

Harold

文書B（eメール2）

From: Harold Chasen
To: Maude Chardin
Date: May 16
Subject: Your office

Dear Maude,
_____
_____
I'd suggest you take the corner office.
_____
_____

Harold

文書C（配置図）

		Office 1	Office 2	
Office 3			Office 4	

10. When will Maude start working?

   (A) On May 16
   (B) On May 17
   (C) In June
   (D) In July

文書Aの情報が必要！

11. In the second e-mail, which office does Harold suggest that Maude should take?

   (A) Office 1
   (B) Office 2
   (C) Office 3
   (D) Office 4

文書Bと文書Cの情報が必要！

次の英文を読み、設問に対する答えとして最も適切なものを（A）～（D）から選びましょう。

Questions 10-14 refer to the following e-mails and layout plan.

From:	Harold Chasen <h.chasen@lifejoy.com>
To:	All staff
Date:	May 16
Subject:	International Marketing

Dear colleagues,

Maude Chardin is joining LifeJoy Products to fill our new position in international marketing. She will be starting work with us from June 1.

Maude is originally from France, but has worked for a number of years in the U.S. and we are delighted to welcome her to the LifeJoy team. Besides English, she is also fluent in Italian and German. If you see her around the building, be sure to welcome her. Her first week will mostly be spent in orientation and she will be guided by Linda to ensure a smooth transition.

Maude's office will be in the trade development section. Her office has not yet been decided, but I'd like her to have close access to Linda's office. I'll send details when this has been confirmed.

Please do your best to make her feel at home. Thanks for joining me in welcoming Maude to the team.

Regards,
Harold Chasen
Human Resources Manager

From:	Harold Chasen <h.chasen@lifejoy.com>
To:	Maude Chardin <marjorie.m.chardin@hashby.co.fr>
Date:	May 16
Subject:	Your office

Dear Maude,

I hope this e-mail finds you well. Everyone here is really looking forward to meeting you next month.

Just a quick note about the options for your office. We're in the process of reorganizing, so you can choose from a few, but I'd recommend you take an office near Linda's. I'd suggest taking the one across from Linda's, with the possibility of moving into Ryan's when his contract ends in May next year.

I've attached a layout plan.

Anyway, let me know if you have any questions, and if you could give me a response by the end of the month, that would be great.

Kind regards,
Harold Chasen
Human Resources Manager

Office 1		Office 3	Linda		
Office 2			Office 4	Ryan	

10. What is the purpose of the first e-mail?

(A) To explain about a new position
(B) To introduce a new member
(C) To extend an invitation to a welcome party
(D) To ask for suggestions for an orientation

11. In the second e-mail, the word "contract" in paragraph 2, line 4, is closest in meaning to

(A) offer
(B) retirement
(C) promotion
(D) agreement

12. What is NOT indicated about Maude?

(A) She can only speak French and English.
(B) Her office has not yet been decided.
(C) She will start working for LifeJoy in June.
(D) She worked in the U.S. for many years.

13. In the second e-mail, what is Maude asked to do?

(A) Take over Ryan's job
(B) Move into Ryan's office in June
(C) Reply by the end of the month
(D) Talk with Linda

14. In the second e-mail, which office does Harold suggest that Maude should take?

(A) Office 1
(B) Office 2
(C) Office 3
(D) Office 4

Communicative Training

Part 7 で取り上げた 2 通の e メールうち、最初の e メールを使ってパートナーと英語で互いに質問をしてみましょう。答える際は、"Yes." や "No." だけで終わらないよう適宜、情報を追加しましょう。

Student A
Student B（パートナー）に下記の質問をしてみましょう。

Student B
Student A（パートナー）の質問に対して Part 7 の英文を見ながら答えましょう。

1. When will Ms. Chardin start her work at LifeJoy Products?

2. What country is she from?

3. Has she ever worked in the U.S.?

4. What languages can she speak besides French?

5. Who will guide her during her first week at LifeJoy Products?

6. Has Ms. Chardin's office been decided yet?

7. (You choose!)

巻末資料

主な接頭辞一覧

接頭辞	意味	例
bi-	2つの（two）	biweekly（隔週の）（< weekly）
dis-	～でない（not）	disregard（無視する）（< regard）
in-, im-, il-, ir- ※ im- は p や m で始まる形容詞、ir- は r で始まる形容詞、il- は l で始まる形容詞の前につくことが多い。	～でない（not）	incomplete（不完全な）（< complete） impossible（不可能な）（< possible） immature（未熟な）（< mature） illegal（不法の）（< legal） irregular（不規則な）（< regular）
mono-	1つの（one）	monorail（モノレール）（< rail）
multi-	多くの（many）	multilingual（多数の言語を使える）（< lingual）
non-	～でない（not）	nonprofit（非営利の）（< profit）
out-	外の（outside） ～以上に（bigger, better, longer, etc.）	outpatient（外来患者）（< patient） outlive（～より長生きする）（< live）
post-	後の（after）	post-tax（〈収入が〉税引き後の）（< tax）
pre-	前の（before）	pre-tax（〈収入が〉税引き前の）（< tax）
re-	再び（again）	reconsider（再考する）（< consider）
semi-	半分（half）	semifinal（準決勝の）（< final）
un-	～でない（not） 元に戻して（back）	unkind（不親切な）（< kind） undo（元に戻す）（< do）

本テキストで取り上げている接尾辞一覧

名詞を作る接尾辞

接尾辞	意味		例
-ant		～する人	applicant（応募者）（< apply）
-ee		～される人	interviewee（面接を受ける人、受験者）（< interview）
-er	人	～する人	interviewer（面接官）（< interview）
-ian		～する人	magician（手品師）（< magic）
-ist		～な人、～する人	specialist（専門家）（< special）
-or		～する人	educator（教育者）（< educate）

接尾辞	意味	例
-ance	こと、状態	compliance（遵守）（< comply）
-ence		existence（存在）（< exist）
-ency		emergency（緊急事態）（< emerge）
-ion, -sion, -tion		invention（発明）（< invent）
-ity, -ty		security（安全）（< secure）
-ment		excitement（興奮）（< excite）
-ness		politeness（礼儀正しさ）（< polite）

動詞を作る接尾辞

接尾辞	意味	例
-ate*	～にする	originate（始まる）（< origin）
-en		widen（～を広くする）（< wide）
-fy, -ify		simplify（単純化する）（< simple）
-ize		specialize（専門にする）（< special）

＊必ずしも動詞とは限らず、fortunate（幸運な）のように形容詞を作る場合もあるので注意が必要。

形容詞を作る接尾辞

接尾辞	意味	例
-able	～できる	imaginable（想像できる）（< imagine）
-al	～の	additional（追加の）（< addition）
-ed	～された	satisfied（満足した）（< satisfy）
-ent	～な	excellent（極めて優れた）（< excel）
-ful	～に満ちた	careful（注意深い）（< care）
-ic	～に関する	atomic（原子の、原子力の）（< atom）
-ical	～に関する	historical（歴史の）（< history）
-ing	～させるような、～している	exciting（興奮させるような）（< excite）
-ive	～な	active（活動的な）（< act）
-less	～のない	careless（不注意な）（< care）
-ory	～な	satisfactory（満足できる）（< satisfy）
-ous	～な	dangerous（危険な）（< danger）

副詞を作る接尾辞

接尾辞	意味	例
-ly*	～なように	specially（特別に）（< special）

＊必ずしも副詞とは限らず、weekly（毎週の）のように形容詞を作る場合もあるので注意が必要。

TEXT PRODUCTION STAFF

edited by	編集
Minako Hagiwara	萩原 美奈子
Takashi Kudo	工藤 隆志

cover design by	表紙デザイン
Nobuyoshi Fujino	藤野 伸芳

illustration by	イラスト
Yoko Sekine	関根 庸子

CD PRODUCTION STAFF

recorded by	吹き込み者
Jack Merluzzi (AmE)	ジャック・マルージ（アメリカ英語）
Rachel Walzer (AmE)	レイチェル・ワルザー（アメリカ英語）
Emma Howard (BrE)	エマ・ハワード（イギリス英語）
Stuart O (AsE)	スチュアート・オー（オーストラリア英語）
Jon Mudryj (CnE)	ジョン・マドレー（カナダ英語）

A COMMUNICATIVE APPROACH TO THE TOEIC® L&R TEST Book 2: Intermediate
コミュニケーションスキルが身に付く TOEIC® L&R TEST《中級編》

2023年1月20日　初版発行
2024年8月30日　第5刷発行

著　者　　角山 照彦　　Simon Capper

発行者　　佐野 英一郎

発行所　　株式会社 成 美 堂
　　　　　〒101-0052　東京都千代田区神田小川町3-22
　　　　　TEL 03-3291-2261　FAX 03-3293-5490
　　　　　https://www.seibido.co.jp

印 刷・製 本　　三美印刷株式会社

ISBN 978-4-7919-7269-2　　　　　　　　　　Printed in Japan